GERMAN
IN 3 MONTHS

Sigrid-B. Martin

**YOUR ESSENTIAL GUIDE TO
UNDERSTANDING AND
SPEAKING GERMAN**

FREE AUDIO APP

THIRD EDITION
Series Editor Elise Bradbury
Senior Editor Amelia Petersen
Senior Art Editor Jane Ewart
Managing Editors Christine Stroyan, Carine Tracanelli
Managing Art Editor Anna Hall
Production Editor Jacqueline Street-Elkayam
Senior Production Controller Samantha Cross
Jacket Project Art Editor Surabhi Wadhwa-Gandhi
Jacket Design Development Manager Sophia MTT
Art Director Karen Self
Associate Publishing Director Liz Wheeler
Publishing Director Jonathan Metcalf

DK INDIA
Project Art Editor Anjali Sachar
Senior DTP Designer Shanker Prasad
Managing Editor Rohan Sinha
Managing Art Editor Sudakshina Basu

This American Edition, 2022
First American Edition, 1990
Published in the United States by DK Publishing
1745 Broadway, 20th Floor, New York, NY 1001

First published in Great Britain by Hugo's Language Books Limited

Copyright © 1990, 2022 Dorling Kindersley Limited
DK, a Division of Penguin Random House LLC
23 24 10 9 8 7 6 5 4 3
003–326924–Jan/2022

Written by
Sigrid-B. Martin
Former lecturer in German
School of European Culture and Languages
University of Kent at Canterbury

A catalog record for this book
is available from the Library of Congress.
ISBN 978-0-7440-5161-2

DK books are available at special discounts when purchased in bulk
for sales promotions, premiums, fund-raising, or educational use.
For details, contact: DK Publishing Special Markets,
1745 Broadway, 20th Floor, New York, NY 10019
SpecialSales@dk.com

Printed and bound in China

For the curious
www.dk.com

MIX
Paper | Supporting
responsible forestry
FSC
www.fsc.org FSC™ C018179

This book was made with Forest Stewardship
Council™ certified paper – one small step
in DK's commitment to a sustainable future.
For more information go to
www.dk.com/our-green-pledge.

Preface

This edition of *Hugo German in 3 Months* was written by Sigrid Martin, whose experience in teaching her native tongue ranges from beginners to post-graduate level. The course is designed for those learning at home who want to acquire a good working knowledge of the language in a short time.

The course begins with an explanation of German pronunciation. Referring to our system of "imitated pronunciation" in the initial weeks of the course will help you learn to understand and pronounce German. However, we strongly encourage you to download the free *DK Hugo in 3 Months* app (see p.5) and to listen to the accompanying audio—this will enable you to pick up the distinctive sounds of the German language. The rest of the course contains the following teaching elements to provide a complete introduction to written and conversational German:

Grammar These sections present the basics of German in a practical way, in an order designed for the learner to make rapid progress. Constructions are clearly explained and examples are included. Listen to the audio to hear the texts pronounced and repeat them out loud. The exercises are designed to consolidate what you've learned as you put the rules into practice.

Vocabulary New words are included in the vocabulary lists: these will help you understand the texts and complete the exercises.

Exercises The exercises will help you remember the rules through applying them. Check your answers against the key at the back of the book. If you make mistakes and don't understand why, go back to the relevant section and read it again.

Conversations The conversations reinforce the points that have been seen as well as introducing idioms and colloquialisms for a thorough grasp of everyday German. We suggest that you listen to the conversations first, then read them aloud and see how closely you can imitate the voices on the recording.

Ideally, you should try to spend about an hour a day on the course, although there is no hard and fast rule on this. Do as much as you feel capable of doing; it's much better to learn a little at a time, and to learn that thoroughly.

Before beginning a new section, always spend ten minutes reviewing what you learned the day before. Then, read each new section carefully, ensuring that you have fully understood the grammar, before listening to the audio to learn the pronunciation of sample sentences and new vocabulary. Finally, complete the exercises at the end of the section. Repeat them until the answers come easily. Repetition is vital to language learning. The more often you listen to a conversation or repeat an oral exercise, the faster your listening skills and fluency in speaking will improve.

When you've completed the course, you should have a very good understanding of the language—more than sufficient for general holiday or business purposes, and enough to lead to language validation tests if this is your eventual goal. We hope you enjoy *Hugo German in 3 Months* and wish you success with your studies!

ACKNOWLEDGMENTS
The author would particularly like to thank her husband, John Martin, for many years the Director of the Institute of Languages and Linguistics at the University of Kent at Canterbury, without whose help she could never have written *Hugo German in 3 Months*. Thanks also to Naomi Laredo, whose expert editing and calming influence in times of stress ensured that the text remained "on track," and to all the others who gave their encouragement and made comments on various drafts of this course.

About the audio app

The audio app that accompanies this German course contains audio recordings for most of the numbered sections, vocabulary boxes, conversations, and exercises.

🔇✕ Where you see this symbol, it indicates that there is no audio for that section.

To start using the audio with this book, first download the *DK Hugo in 3 Months* app on your smartphone or tablet from the App Store or Google Play. Then select German from the list of titles.

Please note that this app is not a stand-alone course. It is designed to be used together with the book, to familiarize you with German speech and to provide examples for you to repeat aloud.

Contents

Week 1

- the German alphabet and spelling
- pronunciation
- the hiatus (pause between two sounds)
- word stress
- German punctuation

1

1.1 SPEAKING GERMAN

Although there are a few sounds in German that will be unfamiliar to English speakers, on the whole the pronunciation is not too tricky to pick up. Don't worry if your pronunciation is less than perfect; the more you practice, the more it will improve.

As you work through the course, listen to the audio and repeat what you hear out loud. Don't be embarrassed to exaggerate the accent; this will help you master the sounds. Whenever you need to, you can refer back to the following explanations and review them.

1.2 THE ALPHABET AND SPELLING

(1) The German alphabet contains all 26 letters of the English alphabet. In addition, three of the vowels have a distinct form with an umlaut (¨) **ä/Ä, ö/Ö, ü/Ü**, which represent entirely different sounds than the same letters without the umlaut.

(2) Note that double **ss** must be written with the letter **ß** (which never starts a word) when the preceding sound is either a long vowel (see section 1.4 [1]) or a vowel combination (see section 1.4 [2]):

Kuss	*but*	**Gruß**
floss	*but*	**Floß**
blass	*but*	**fraß**
	and	**Fleiß**
		Strauß
		äußern

(3) All nouns, not just names, begin with a capital letter. The pronoun **Sie**, the formal word for "you" (see section 3.2), and related formal pronouns (e.g., **Ihr** "your") always begin with a capital. But unlike in English, the first-person singular pronoun ("I") starts with a lowercase letter (**ich**).

(4) Here are the letters of the alphabet and how they are said out loud, shown in our system of imitated pronunciation (see the following sections). This will be useful if you have to spell out a word.

A	<u>ah</u>	**J**	yot	**S**	es
B	b<u>eh</u>	**K**	k<u>ah</u>	**T**	t<u>eh</u>
C	ts<u>eh</u>	**L**	el	**U**	<u>oo</u>
D	d<u>eh</u>	**M**	em	**V**	fow
E	<u>eh</u>	**N**	en	**W**	v<u>eh</u>
F	ef	**O**	<u>oh</u>	**X**	iks
G	g<u>eh</u>	**P**	p<u>eh</u>	**Y**	<u>ue</u>pseelon
H	h<u>ah</u>	**Q**	k<u>oo</u>	**Z**	tset
I	<u>ee</u>	**R**	er		

1.3 PRONUNCIATION

There is greater consistency between the way a word is spelled and how it's pronounced in German than in English, making German more phonetic. However, some letters are pronounced differently from the same letters in English, and others appear in unfamiliar combinations, so we'll focus on these in the next sections. Listen to the audio and repeat each of the examples aloud.

Note that no English meanings are given for the examples in this first week of the course. The goal here is just to concentrate on the sounds of the words, so resist the temptation to wonder what they mean for the moment.

The following letters are pronounced differently from their English equivalents, or their pronunciation can vary, depending on their position in a word.

Imitated pronunciation

b	[b],	[p]	At the start of words and syllables, these
d	[d],	[t]	are pronounced as in English. At the end
g	[g],	[k]	of words and syllables (standing either
	[*h*],	[*k*]	alone or in a cluster of consonants of

which they may not be the final letter), **b** is pronounced as **p**, **d** as **t**, and **g** as **k** (or **ch**): this means that the end of **habt** sounds like **klappt**; that **wird** sounds exactly the same as **Wirt**; **Rad** is pronounced like **Rat**; **Erdöl** sounds like **Ert-öl**; **folg** sounds like **Volk**; and **Krieg** like **kriek**. (Most of these words actually exist and some are therefore homophones: words that are spelled differently but sound alike.)

c   is principally used in the combinations **ch** and **ck** but is rarely found on its own except in foreign words.

j [y]   is almost always pronounced like the English y at the start of a word (e.g., "yet," "young"), as in **Junge, Jammer**.

q   is always followed by a **u**, but the combination is pronounced differently than in English and is similar to k + v in rapid succession, as in **quer, Quatsch, Qualität**.

s [s], [z]   As in English, **s** is pronounced in two different ways: like the s sound in "sits" and "its," or like the z sound in "busy" and "is." However, note that whereas in English the s sound occurs at the start of words or syllables, and the z sound usually occurs at the end, the opposite is the case in German. The German **s** is always pronounced like z at the start of a word (except in the combinations **sp** and **st**, see below) and like s at the end of words and syllables.

Here are some examples:
<u>like z</u>
sein, Symbol, Absicht (Ab|sicht), Fürsorge (Für|sorge), Rose (Ro|se), Riese (Rie|se)

<u>like s</u>
Gast, längst, Wespe (Wes|pe), Muster (Mus|ter), meins, meines (mei|nes)

Words containing both sounds:
süß, seins, seines (sei|nes), dieses (die|ses)

[sh]   **s** in the combinations **sp** and **st** at the start of words and syllables is pronounced like the English "sh":
Speck, spät, spülen, gespannt (ge|spannt), Stamm, sterben, Strecke, steigen, erstaunt (er|staunt), verstimmt (ver|stimmt), Anstand (An|stand)

th [t]   is never like "th" in "this" or "thing," but pronounced simply as t. Found only in words of foreign origin, for example:
Apotheke, Hypothek, Thymian, These

tion [tsiohn]   is found only in the many imported words ending in **-tion**, such as:
Station, Aktion, Funktion, Tradition

v [f]   is almost always pronounced f as in "from": **Vater, von, Verlag, bevor**

w [v] is like the v in "very," for example: **was, Wein, Weg, Wirt**

y [ue] is pronounced as a vowel, not a consonant, and sounds like the German (short) vowel **ü** (see section 1.4), as in: **System, sympatisch**

z [ts] is NEVER like the English z as in "hazard," but like t + s spoken in rapid succession, almost simultaneously, often with no more than a trace of the t. Something similar is found in the usual English pronunciation of "Mozart," although in German this sound can also start a word, which can seem very odd to English speakers. Examples: **Zeit, zu, Zinsen, Zange, Zorn, zusammen, beizeiten, inzwischen (in|zwischen), Weizen (Wei|zen), Schnauze (Schnau|ze), Konzert, Winzer, Geiz, Sitz, Franz, Holz, Harz, Lenz**

Unfamiliar groups of consonants, or consonants in unfamiliar places in words, can look intimidating, even if the individual sounds are not necessarily difficult to pronounce.

It can be helpful to learn these combinations and the corresponding pronunciation as "blocks."

dsch [dj] is pronounced like the j in "jump." It is quite rare and only used in certain foreign words: **Dschungel, Dschihad, Dschunke**

gd [kt] is pronounced "kt," like the end of "flicked." It is fairly rare, although the first example is a frequent word: **Jagd, Magd**

hd, hl(t), hm(t), hn(t), hr(t), ht	This **h** is not pronounced; it just indicates that the preceding vowel is pronounced as a long vowel (see section 1.4). Similarly, ignore the **h** between vowels, except in compound words: **Fehde, Mehl, wählt, lahm, rahmt, kühn, wohnt, wahr, lehrt, weht, sehen, ruhen** BUT **Seehafen (See|hafen), bleihaltig (blei|haltig)**
ng	When this combination occurs between vowels, the g is barely vocalized, as in "singer": **Anger, Finger, Hunger**
pf	Whether at the beginning or end of words and syllables, the p + f are spoken in rapid succession, almost simultaneously, often with no more than a trace of the p: **Pfeil, Pferd, Pfund, Dampfer, impfen, Kupfer, Sumpf, Krampf, glimpflich**
sch, schl, schm, schn, schr, schw	**sch** is like "sh" in "shut" or "wish," whether at the start or end of words and syllables. Note that **sch** + a consonant is only found at the beginning of words: **Schande, Rausch, Schlampe, schmelzen, Schnauze, Schraube, schwitzen**
tsch [ch]	is like "ch" in "cheap," "much," or "match." It can be found at the start of a word but is more frequently in the middle or end: **tschüs, Tscheche, Matsch, futsch, Deutschland, Rutsch**
tz [ts]	This only occurs in the middle or at the end of words. It sounds like the "ts" in "gets," or like the German **z**: **plötzlich, platzen, sitzen, Fritz, Gesetz**

zw [tsv]   This is like t + s + v spoken in rapid
succession and occurs only at the start
of words and syllables:
**Zwang, bezwingen (be|zwingen),
Zwerg, zwei, inzwischen
(in|zwischen), Zweck**

1.4 VOWELS AND VOWEL COMBINATIONS

Though there are only eight letters that represent vowels
in German (the five in the English alphabet, plus **ä, ö, ü**),
there are twice as many vowel sounds, because each
can be pronounced either as a long or a short vowel.
(This refers to the duration, or length, of the vowel
sound—long vowels are drawn out more.)

This distinction is important to master, as it can make a
big difference in making yourself understood. The spelling
can sometimes provide a clue to knowing whether a
vowel is long or short.

The pronunciation of a vowel is long if:
- the vowel is doubled: **Beet, Saat, Boot**
- the vowel is followed by **h**:
  Bahn, Huhn, Lohn
- the vowel **i** is followed by **e**:
  fies, mies, Grieß
- the vowel is followed by **ß**:
  Maß, bloß, Muße, Füße, Blöße, Maße

The pronunciation of a vowel is short if:
- the vowel is followed by a doubled consonant
  or by **ck**:
  Hütte, Affe, Zweck
- the vowel is followed by **ss**:
  blass, Ross, muss
- the vowel is followed by **ng**:
  Rang, jung, ging

1

Detailed pronunciation tips for each vowel sound follow, but keep in mind that trying to describe pronunciations in terms of English sounds can only provide approximations and are not a substitute for listening to German. Make sure to listen to the examples in the audio and repeat them out loud.

One general guideline is to try to pronounce German single-sound vowels with a greater sharpness and energy than English vowels.

(1) Single vowels

long **a**   [ah]   This is pronounced in a similar way to the "ah" in the words "father" or "barn."

short **a**   [ah]   This is a shorter a, as in "fat" or "track."

Bahn/Bann, Kahn/kann, Wahn/wann, kam/Kamm, mahn/Mann, Saat/satt

long **e**   [eh]   This is pronounced like the "ay" or "eh" sound in "lane" or "drape."

short **e**   [e]   This is a shorter e, as in "get" or "crept."

Beet/Bett, wen/wenn, den/denn, hehl/hell, fehl/Fell, gehl/gell

long **i(e)**   [ee]   This is pronounced like the "ee" sound in "keen" or "lean."

short **i**   [i]   This is a shorter i, as in "fit" or "clip."

ihm/im, schief/Schiff, Stil/still, rief/Riff, siech/sich, mies/miss

long **o**   [oh]   This is pronounced like the "oh" sound in "home" or "bone."

short **o** [o] This is a shorter o, as in "shot" or "crop."

Hof/hoff, Ofen/offen, wohne/Wonne, Wohle/Wolle

long **u** [oo] This is pronounced like the "oo" sound in "moon" or "doom."

short **u** [oo] This is a shorter u, as in "put" or "foot."

Pute/Putte, Ruhm/Rum, Kruke/Krucke, Mus/muss

long **ä** [e] This is pronounced like "ay" in "lane," but more open—in between "lane" and "leg."

short **ä** [e] This sounds just like the German **e**: "let"

käme/Kämme, stähle/Ställe, Pfähle/Fälle, wähle/Wälle

long **ö** [oe] Say the long **e** ("eh") while rounding and protruding the lips.

short **ö** [oe] Say the short **e** ("e") while rounding and protruding the lips. Both are similar to the tight, pursed vowel in the French *œuvre*.

Höhle/Hölle, Flöße/flösse

long **ü** [ue] Say the long **i(e)** ("ee") while rounding and protruding the lips.

short **ü** [ue] Say the short **i** ("i") while rounding and protruding the lips. Both are similar to the tight, pursed vowel in the French *une*.

Wüste/wüsste, Hüte/Hütte, fühlen/füllen, führst/Fürst

(2) Diphthongs

Diphthongs (vowel combinations that glide from one vowel sound to another) are always drawn out rather than short. The three diphthongs below resemble vowel combinations in English, but they will sound more German if you move your tongue (and jaw) in a more pronounced way.

ai/ei   [y]   This sounds similar to the word "eye"— think "Einstein":
Hain, Mai, Kai, weiß, Kleid, weich

au   [ow]   This sounds similar to the "ow" diphthong in "cow" or "mouth":
Raum, Zaun, Maul, Haus, Haut, Raub

äu/eu   [oy]   This sounds similar to the "oy" diphthong in "void" or "annoy":
häuft, läuft, Säume, deutet, freut, neun

(3) Unstressed syllables containing **e** or **er**

There are also many words with an unstressed vowel sound that is similar to the initial a in "about."

[ɐ]   Unstressed syllables containing the vowel **e** have a sound similar to that in "the." It is a sort of neutral "uh" sound, but with a trace of the short **e** as in "get":
Befund, Gericht, waagerecht, Hilferuf

The above is especially true if the **e** ends a word. In this case, the final **e** is barely audible. Just the hint of an "uh" is voiced:
Hilfe, welche, Menge, ihre

An unstressed **e** is barely audible even if followed by a consonant (other than **r**):
Hall_e_nbad, Spieg_e_lei, Dank_e_sbrief, deut_e_t

[uh]   Unstressed syllables ending in **er** are pronounced in a similar way to the English pronunciation; the **r** is NOT pronounced, resembling an "uh" sound:
Wied_er_kehr, Kind_er_wagen, Mess_er_kante, bess_er_, hell_er_, ihr_er_

The same sound, only lengthened, occurs if the **er** is followed by **n**. Again, the **r** is NOT pronounced:
gest_ern_, Brüd_ern_, and_ern_falls, kent_ern_

Along with the audio, listen to and practice the distinction between **e** and **er**, and between **en** and **ern**, in the following pairs of words:

Ehe/eher, Feste/fester, Silbe/Silber, Güte/Güter, Lehren/Lehrern, wischen/Wischern, Wäschen/Wäschern

1.5 CONSONANTS

As mentioned in section 1.3, most of the consonants are fairly straightforward for English speakers to pronounce. The only three consonants that are quite different from English sounds are **ch**, **l**, and **r**.

ch   This letter combination can have two radically different pronunciations, neither of which occurs in English:

(1)   [*h*]   When **ch** follows the vowels **e, ei, eu, i, ie, ä, äu, ü** or a consonant, it sounds

something like the initial h in "Hugo" or "human" aspirated very forcefully. Force the air through the mouth, drawing out the h sound:

Blech, Reich, Seuche, mich, riechen, Bäche, Bäuche, Küche, Storch, Dolch, durch

The same sound is used in three common words of foreign origin, **Chemie, China, Chirurg**, and at the start of the diminutive ending **-chen** (conveying "little ..."):

Mädchen, Riemchen, Häuschen, Küsschen, Gläschen, Frauchen

It is also a common pronunciation of the consonant **g**, either alone or with other consonants, when it is at the end of a word or syllable following any of the vowels or diphthongs listed for the [*h*] pronunciation of **g**. It is an alternative to pronouncing the final **g** as a **k** (see section 1.3):

wichtig, grantig, Predigt, gütig

(2) [k] When **ch** follows **a, au, o, u**, it is a guttural sound similar to the Scottish pronunciation of "loch" (think of the German pronunciation of "Bach"). It is made by tensing the back of the throat while forcing the breath through it:

auch, Bach, Suche, Loch, brauchen, Sucht, machen

l

In English, there are a range of subtly different pronunciations of l according to its position in a word and the surrounding letters. There is only one sound for the German l, however, whatever its context.

The closest parallels in English are the sounds in "clean," "leek," and "language" (although not exactly), whereas those in "vault," "feel," "Oliver," "culvert," and "apple" are different from the German sound.
The tip of the tongue should be placed against the upper gum and the tongue kept flat:

lieb, leben, lang, laut, Leute; Klippe, Klang, Flamme, klug, Flucht; goldig, Walzer, älter, albern, ulkig; belebt, Brille, Rolle, völlig; fällig; Esel, fühl, voll, wohl, Stahl; wedelt, wählt, Silber, Felder, Helm

r

The letter **r** (although not pronounced in the combination **er**, see section 1.4) is "gargled." This sound is made at the back of the throat like **ch**, but with less breath forced through. It sounds a little like the French guttural r.

r is pronounced in this way:

- at the start of a word:
  Rand, rund, Rasen, Riese
- after another consonant at the start of a word:
  Frau, grün, Gras, Gruß

■ between vowels or diphthongs in the middle of words:
Beere, Fähre, Karre, mürrisch, waren

r is not pronounced as a consonant but as a neutral vowel sound similar to the vowel glide in British English, lengthening the preceding vowel, when it is:

■ alone at the end of a word or syllable:
besser, woher, war, klar, Herr, Meer, mehr, fror, gar, wurde, warte, würdig (note that **Narr** is an exception and has the consonant sound)
■ before another consonant at the end of a word or syllable:
Schwert, Wurst, Herz, warnte, horchte

1.6 THE HIATUS

Whereas in English, words are often run together so that a word beginning with a vowel is linked to the preceding word with the final consonant acting as a bridge, this does not occur in German.

Words beginning with a vowel are preceded with a hiatus, which is a brief pause between two sounds. In English, you can sometimes hear this pause between two vowel sounds: for example, in the words "reelect" or "cooperate," or in the expression "Uh oh!"

In German, this pause also occurs within compound words or words with a prefix before a vowel:
mach * aus, im * Auge, hau * ab, Vor*arbeiter, miss*-achten, ge*einigt, im * Ofen, würde * ich * auch

Compare the pronunciation of **hau * ab** with the English "How are you?" or **Vor*arbeiter** with "for ages."

The rhythm of a language has a lot to do with where the stress falls in syllables and within sentences. In German words, the stress usually falls on the first syllable, although there are many exceptions.

One reliable rule is that whereas all English words starting with "un-" are unstressed on that first syllable, such words in German put the stress on the **un-**: **un**glücklich, **un**erfahren, **un**freundlich, **un**geduldig

As we will be discovering, in German it is possible—and common—to create compound words out of smaller word units. In these compound words, the stress is on the stressed syllable of the first word unit: **krei**deweiß, **Plat**tenspieler, **Bril**lenetui, **Stu**dentenwohnheim (kreide|weiß, Platten|spieler, Brillen|etui, Studenten|wohn|heim)

Most of the exceptions to the rule of the stress on the first syllable are either words of foreign origin or words containing specifically unstressed first syllables or prefixes (see section 9.7):

foreign words:
kontrol**lie**ren, telefo**nie**ren, Ma**schi**ne, Pa**ket**, offi**ziell**

unstressed prefixes:
be|**spre**chen, miss|**brau**chen, ver|**ra**ten, ge|**lin**gen, er|**rö**ten

However, some short words in frequent use are also exceptions, while combinations with **da-** and **wo-** (see sections 8.8 and 11.4) are usually not stressed on the **da-** or **wo-**:
je**doch**, so**gar**, da**mit**, da**zu**, da**ne**ben, wo**rauf**, in**zwi**schen

In the imitated pronunciation, the stressed syllable is always printed in bold type. You can also refer to a German dictionary to check where the word stress falls as well as pronunciation.

1.8 PUNCTUATION

In German, you will notice that commas sometimes appear where they would not be used in English. This has to do with rules regarding separating clauses. In the two English examples below, the commas or lack of commas convey different meanings:

My sister, who hates noise, ended up staying in a hotel next to a night club.
The woman who called yesterday was a friend of my sister's.

But in German, in the second sentence, there would have to be commas following "woman" and "yesterday" in line with the punctuation rules for clauses. Just be aware of this—commas in German have a more strict grammatical function rather than denoting meaning.

The punctuation used for quoted speech is also different from English usage (see section 13.7), and colons are used more often—to introduce short inserts in the middle of sentences, for example. Exclamation marks are also used more frequently than in English.

Week 2

- *greetings and useful everyday phrases*
- *two key differences with English: inflection and word order*
- *the definite article **der, die, das** ("the") and how its form varies according to the gender of the noun it refers to and whether the noun is singular or plural*
- *how to form the plural of nouns*

2.1 WORD ENDINGS AND WORD ORDER

(1) When the form of a word changes (typically the ending) to express a grammatical function or some other attribute, such as number or gender, this is called inflection. German is a much more highly inflected language than English: several forms may be possible for words that are invariable in English.

(2) The word order in a German sentence is often different from the word order in English. "I can't find the key because it's too dark" would be "I can the key not find because it too dark is" or "The key can I not find because it too dark is."

These two key differences between the languages will be introduced gradually throughout the course. Don't worry!

2.2 GREETINGS AND EVERYDAY PHRASES

Throughout Germany, the most common greeting during the daytime is **Guten Tag!** (Good day!) (or, in the morning, **Guten Morgen!**). In the evening people, say **Guten Abend!** In southern Germany and Austria, **Grüß Gott!** is usual at any time of day. All these are often accompanied by a handshake, even within the family.

After the greeting, one person will often add **Wie geht's?** or **Wie geht's Ihnen?** (How are you?), to which the response is usually **Danke, gut**, or **Gut, danke** (Fine, thanks), or simply **Danke**.

IMITATED PRONUNCIATION

goo-ten t<u>ah</u>k; **goo**-ten **moe**-gen; **goo**-ten **ah**-bent;
grues got; v<u>ee</u> g<u>eh</u>ts **ee**-nen; **dahng**-ke g<u>oo</u>t

Exercise 1

Practice saying the sentences in this dialogue until you feel comfortable with them.

Two hard-up customers at a refreshment kiosk

KUNDE	Guten Tag!
BESITZERIN	Guten Tag! Bitte schön …?
KUNDE	Zwei Cola und eine Wurst mit Brot, bitte.
BESITZERIN	Was? Sie wollen zwei Cola aber nur eine Wurst?
KUNDE	Ja …, das heißt, ja und nein. Wie teuer ist eine Wurst?
BESITZERIN	Nur drei Euro.
KUNDE	Na gut, dann zwei Cola und zweimal Wurst mit Brot.
BESITZERIN	Bitte schön … Zehn Euro zusammen.
KUNDE	Danke schön. Auf Wiedersehen!
BESITZERIN	Auf Wiedersehen!

Translation

CUSTOMER	Hello!
MANAGER	Hello! Yes, can I help you?
CUSTOMER	Two colas and one hotdog (lit. "sausage with bread"), please.
MANAGER	What? You want two colas but only one hotdog (lit. "sausage")?
CUSTOMER	Yes … I mean yes and no. How much is a hotdog?
MANAGER	Only three euros.
CUSTOMER	All right, then two colas and hotdogs.
MANAGER	Here you are … ten euros altogether.
CUSTOMER	Thank you. Goodbye!
MANAGER	Goodbye!

In our first example of inflection in German, there are a total of six words for "the": **der, die, das, den, dem, des**. It is always a three-letter word starting with **d-** , plus an ending that can depend on three factors. The first of these factors is the gender of the noun.

All German nouns are either masculine (m.), feminine (f.), or neuter (n.). This is the case of nouns that refer to people, but it's also the case for objects. When you learn a new noun, try to remember its gender, as this affects certain other words used with the noun in a sentence.

When a singular noun is the subject of the sentence, the definite article "the" is **der** (for a masculine noun), **die** (for a feminine noun), or **das** (for a neuter noun):

Der Junge (m.) ist krank. The boy is ill.
 so <u>der</u> **Junge**
Der Preis (m.) ist hoch. The price is high.
 so <u>der</u> **Preis**
Die Tante (f.) ist freundlich. The aunt is kind.
 so <u>die</u> **Tante**
Die Farbe (f.) ist dunkel. The color is dark.
 so <u>die</u> **Farbe**
Das Kind (n.) ist nett. The child is nice.
 so <u>das</u> **Kind**
Das Haus (n.) ist alt. The house is old.
 so <u>das</u> **Haus**

IMITATED PRONUNCIATION

deh-uh **yoong**-*e* ist krahnk; deh-uh prys; h<u>oh</u>*k*;
d<u>ee</u> **tan**-t*e*; **froynt**-li*h*; d<u>ee</u> **fah**-b*e*; **doong**-k*e*l; dahs kint;
net; das hows; ahlt

Exercise 2

Learn the lists of words in **A** about house and family, saying each word with **der, die**, or **das** in front of it.

Then, cover up the lists and read out the words in **B**, giving each word the correct definite article (**der, die**, or **das**) and checking that you know the meaning.

Finally, cover up **B** and give the German words preceded by **der, die**, or **das** for each English word listed in **C**.

(NOTE: We won't include this type of exercise again, but you could devise a similar exercise for yourself with each new set of words each week.)

A

m. (der)		f. (die)		n. (das)	
Mann	man/ husband	Frau	woman/ wife	Kind	child
				Mädchen	girl
Vater	father	Mutter	mother	Haus	house
Sohn	son	Tochter	daughter	Zimmer	room
Bruder	brother	Schwester	sister	Fenster	window
Wirt	landlord	Wirtin	landlady	Bett	bed
Tisch	table	Küche	kitchen	Wasser	water
Stuhl	chair	Tür	door	Auto	car
Schrank	cupboard	Zeitung	newspaper	Buch	book
Flur	hall	Uhr	clock	Messer	knife
Hund	dog	Katze	cat		

B

Auto, Fenster, Wirt, Uhr, Tochter, Haus, Flur, Messer, Tür, Hund, Küche, Katze, Bruder, Mann, Kind, Zeitung, Sohn, Schwester, Stuhl, Buch, Wirtin, Schrank, Frau, Bett, Vater, Zimmer, Mutter, Wasser, Mädchen, Tisch

C

book, knife, sister, door, newspaper, woman, room, landlord, car, table, water, clock, house, window, child, cupboard, girl, cat, kitchen, father, dog, brother, daughter, hall, mother, chair, son, man, landlady, bed

IMITATED PRONUNCIATION:

mahn; **fah**-tuh; z<u>oh</u>n; **broo**-duh; vi*er*t; tish; sht<u>oo</u>l;
shrahnk; fl<u>oo</u>-uh; hoont; frow; **moo**-tuh; to*k*-tuh; **shves**-
tuh; **vi*er***-tin; **kue**-*he*; t<u>ue</u>-uh; **tsy**-toong; <u>oo</u>-uh; **kaht**-s*e*;
kint; **m*e*t**-*he*n; hows; **tsi**-muh; **fens**-tuh; bet; **vah**-suh;
ow-t<u>oh</u>; b<u>oo</u>*k*; **me**-suh

2.4 THE PLURAL FORM OF "THE"

When the noun refers to more than one thing, **die** is
always used for "the," regardless of gender:

die $\left\lbrace\begin{array}{l}\textbf{Preise sind hoch} \\ \textbf{Farben sind dunkel} \\ \textbf{Häuser sind alt}\end{array}\right.$ the $\left\lbrace\begin{array}{l}\text{prices are high} \\ \text{colors are dark} \\ \text{houses are old}\end{array}\right.$

Here's a summary:

singular			plural
m.	f.	n.	m. f. n.
der	**die**	**das**	**die**

IMITATED PRONUNCIATION

deh-uh; d<u>ee</u>; dahs; d<u>ee</u>

2.5 FORMING THE PLURAL OF NOUNS

In English, nouns generally inflect to show the plural by
adding -s (although there are variations). In German, there
are various ways to form the plural of a noun. Here are
some basic guidelines, but it's a good idea to try to learn
the plural form when you encounter a new noun:

(1) Feminine nouns usually add **-n** or **-en** to the singular:

Küche kitchen → **Küchen** kitchens
Zeitung newspaper → **Zeitungen** newspapers
Frau woman → **Frauen** women

But other plural forms for feminine words are possible (e.g., the addition of an umlaut, changing the vowel sound, or **-nen**):

Mutter mother → **Mütter** mothers
Tochter daughter → **Töchter** daughters
Wirtin landlady → **Wirtinnen** landladies

(2) Masculine and neuter nouns often add:

-e	**Hund** dog → **Hunde** dogs
-en	**Bett** bed → **Betten** beds
-er	**Kind** child → **Kinder** children

and any of these endings may be accompanied by a change in the sound of certain vowels:

-a-	**Mann** man → **Männer** men
-o-	**Sohn** son → **Söhne** sons
-u-	**Stuhl** chair → **Stühle** chairs
-au-	**Haus** house → **Häuser** houses

(3) Some masculine and neuter nouns don't change at all:

Zimmer → **Zimmer** room, rooms
Messer → **Messer** knife, knives

(4) Some masculine and neuter nouns only have a change in the vowel sound, which adds an umlaut to indicate this:

Vater father → **Väter** fathers
Bruder brother → **Brüder** brothers

(5) Some words taken from other languages add **-s**:

Auto car → **Autos** cars

Exercise 3

A lists the words you learned in Exercise 2, but they are now shown first with the plural abbreviation used in dictionaries* and then in the full plural form. Learn these, then cover up **A** and try to say the plurals of all the singular words in list **B**.

A

Mann (⁻er)	Männer	Frau (-en)	Frauen
Vater (⁻)	Väter	Mutter (⁻)	Mütter
Sohn (⁻e)	Söhne	Tochter (⁻)	Töchter
Bruder (⁻)	Brüder	Schwester (-n)	Schwestern
Wirt (-e)	Wirte	Wirtin (-nen)	Wirtinnen
Tisch (-e)	Tische	Küche (-n)	Küchen
Stuhl (⁻e)	Stühle	Tür (-en)	Türen
Schrank (⁻e)	Schränke	Zeitung (-en)	Zeitungen
Flur (-e)	Flure	Uhr (-en)	Uhren
Hund (-e)	Hunde	Katze (-n)	Katzen
Kind (-er)	Kinder	Bett (-en)	Betten
Mädchen (-)	Mädchen	Wasser	No plural
Haus (⁻er)	Häuser	Auto (-s)	Autos
Zimmer (-)	Zimmer	Buch (⁻er)	Bücher
Fenster (-)	Fenster	Messer (-)	Messer

*In following word lists and in the mini-dictionary at the end of the course, the plural of each noun is given by the appropriate abbreviation in parentheses.

B Auto, Fenster, Wirt, Uhr, Tochter, Haus, Flur, Messer, Tür, Hund, Küche, Katze, Bruder, Mann, Kind, Zeitung, Sohn, Schwester, Stuhl, Buch, Wirtin, Schrank, Frau, Bett, Vater, Zimmer, Mutter, Mädchen, Tisch

IMITATED PRONUNCIATION

me-nuh; **fe**-tuh; **zoe**-n*e*; **brue**-duh; **vier**-t*e*; **ti**-sh*e*; **shtue**-l*e*; **shreng**-k*e*; **floo**-r*e*; **hoon**-d*e*; **kin**-duh; **met**-*he*n; **hoy**-zuh; **tsi**-muh; **fens**-tuh; **frow**-*e*n; **mue**-tuh; **toeh**-tuh; **shves**-tuhn; **vier**-ti-n*e*n; **kue**-*he*n; **tue**-ren; **tsy**-toong-*e*n; **oo**-r*e*n; **kaht**-s*e*n; **be**-t*e*n; **ow**-t<u>ohs</u>; **bue**-*h*uh; **me**-suh

Week 3

- *grammatical case and declension in German*
- *the definite article ("the") and case*
- *personal pronouns ("I" and "me," "we" and "us," etc.)*
- *the present tense of* **sein** *("to be") and* **haben** *("to have")*
- *the present tense conjugations of regular verbs such as* **machen** *("to make")*

3.1 GRAMMATICAL CASE AND DECLENSION

So far, we've seen that the form of the definite article **der**, **die**, or **das** depends on:
(1) gender (m./f./n.)
(2) number (singular/plural)

The third factor that affects the form is grammatical case. Case is a way of marking certain words according to their function in a sentence. Compare the below:

A **Der Hund ist harmlos.** The dog is harmless.
B **Der Junge liebt den Hund.** The boy loves the dog.

In A the dog is the subject of the sentence, while in B the boy is the subject, and the dog has become the direct object of the action. In German, if a noun is the subject of a sentence, it is in the nominative case. If it is the direct object, it is in the accusative case. Certain words in the sentence related to the noun change form according to the case to reflect their role. This is called declension.

To help you get used to this concept, we indicate the nominative case as subject (SU) and the accusative as direct object (DO) so that you can make the direct link with their role. Below are the declensions for the definite article in these two cases. Note that only the masculine singular changes.

	singular			plural
	m.	f.	n.	m. f. n.
SU	**der**	**die**	**das**	**die**
DO	**den**	**die**	**das**	**die**

3.2 PERSONAL PRONOUNS

Personal pronouns can also decline according to case.

Nominative (SU)	Accusative (DO)
ich I	**mich** me
du you (informal singular)	**dich** you
er he	**ihn** him
sie she	**sie** her
es it	**es** it
wir we	**uns** us
ihr you (informal plural)	**euch** you
sie they	**sie** them
Sie you (formal: sing. & pl.)	**Sie** you

German also has different forms of "you" for the informal, formal, singular, and plural (see sections 7.5 and 13.3.)

3.3 USEFUL VERBS: "TO BE," "TO HAVE," AND "TO MAKE"

As in many languages, some of the most common verbs are also irregular. This is the case of both **sein** (to be) and **haben** (to have), which you will be using frequently, so it's a good idea to learn their conjugations early on.

Here they are in the present tense. Note that in German, the present tense can be used for the simple present ("I talk") as well as the present continuous ("I am talking").

sein (to be)

ich bin I am
du bist you are (informal singular)
er/sie/es ist he/she/it is
wir sind we are
ihr seid you are (informal plural)
sie sind they are
Sie sind you are (formal: singular & plural)

(Note that there are different verb conjugations for the different forms of "you.")

3

haben (to have)

ich habe I have
du hast you have (informal singular)
er/sie/es hat he/she/it has
wir haben we have
ihr habt you have (informal plural)
sie haben they have
Sie haben you have (formal: singular & plural)

The following useful verb has a regular conjugation pattern.

machen (to make, to do)

ich mache I make, do
du machst you make, do (informal singular)
er/sie/es macht he/she/it makes, does
wir machen we make, do
ihr macht you make, do (informal plural)
sie machen they make, do
Sie machen you make, do (formal: singular & plural)

To form the present tense of regular verbs, the **-en** ending is removed from the infinitive (e.g., **machen**), and the following endings are added to the stem (e.g., **mach-**):

1st person singular (I)	**-e**
2nd person singular (you, informal)	**-st**
3rd person singular (he, she, it)	**-t**
	-et for stems ending in **-d** or **-t**
1st person plural (we)	**-en**
2nd person plural (you, informal)	**-t**
3rd person plural (they)	**-en**
Formal, sing. & pl. (you)	**-en**

IMITATED PRONUNCIATION

zyn; bin; bist; ist; zint; zyd; **hah**-ben; **hah**-be; hast; haht; hapt; **mah**-ken; **mah**-ke; mahkst; mahkt; (Ex.) **lee**-ben; **kow**-fen; **mah**-ken; **hoh**-len; **roo**-fen; **ko**-men; **bring**-en; **tring**-ken

Exercise 1

A Learn the following verbs and then translate the sentences in **B**:

lieben	to love
kaufen	to buy
machen	to make, to do
holen	to fetch, to go and get
rufen	to call
kommen	to come
bringen	to bring
trinken	to drink

B Translate into German:

1 The father loves the landlady.

2 It is harmless!

3 He buys the newspaper.

4 She makes the beds.

5 The daughter fetches the car.

6 She calls the cat and the dog.

7 The cat and the dog come.

8 The landlady brings water.

9 Father, landlady, daughter, dog, and cat drink the water.

VOCABULARY

Here are some new words that you'll discover in the conversation that follows. The plural form of nouns is given in parentheses.

	Entschuldigung!	Excuse me!
	suchen	to look for
die	**Touristeninformation**	tourist information office
	liegen	to be (located)
	am	in/on the
der	**Theaterplatz**	Theater Square
	Wie?	How?
	dahin	(to) there

	nicht	not
	leicht	easy
	Moment mal	just a moment
	gehen	to go
	über	over, across
die	**Kreuzung (-en)**	crossroads
	zweite	second
die	**Straße (-n)**	street
	rechts	on the right
der	**Marktplatz (¨e)**	marketplace
	sehen	to see
	dann	then
die	**Kirche (-n)**	church
das	**Gasthaus (¨er)**	inn
die	**Rose (-n)**	rose
	nehmen	to take
	zwischen	between
	eins	one
	zwei	two
	drei	three
	vierte	fourth
	immer geradeaus	straight ahead
	für	for
	etwa	about, approximately
	fünfhundert	five hundred
der	**Meter (-)**	meter
	finden	to find
	sofort	immediately
	furchtbar	terribly
	schwierig	difficult
	es macht nichts	it doesn't matter
	um	at (time of day)
	dieser	this
die	**Zeit (-en)**	time
	sowieso	anyway
	geschlossen	closed

IMITATED PRONUNCIATION

ent-**shool**-di-goonk; **zoo**-k<u>e</u>n; d<u>ee</u> t<u>oo</u>-**ris**-t<u>e</u>n*in-fo<u>e</u>-mah-
tsi<u>ohn</u>; **lee**-g<u>e</u>n; ahm; deh-uh t<u>e</u>h-**ah**-tuh-plahts; v<u>ee</u>;
dah-**hin**; ni<u>h</u>t; ly<u>h</u>t; m<u>oh</u>-**ment** mahl; **geh**-<u>e</u>n; **ue**-buh;
d<u>ee</u> **kroy**-tsung; **tsvy**-t<u>e</u>; d<u>ee</u> **shtrah**-s<u>e</u>, re<u>h</u>ts; deh-uh
m<u>a</u>hkt-plahts; **zeh**-<u>e</u>n; dahn; d<u>ee</u> **kee**-uh-<u>h</u>e, dahs
gahst-hows; d<u>ee</u> **r<u>oh</u>**-z<u>e</u>; **neh**-m<u>e</u>n; **tsvi**-sh<u>e</u>n; yns; tsvy;
dry; **fee**-uh-t<u>e</u>; **i**-muh g<u>e</u>-**r<u>ah</u>**-d<u>e</u>*ows; f<u>ue</u>-uh; **et**-vah;
fuenf-hoon-duht; deh-uh **meh**-tuh; **fin**-d<u>e</u>n; z<u>oh</u>-**fo<u>e</u>rt**;
foo<u>e</u>rht-b<u>ah</u>; **shvee**-ri<u>h</u>; es mah<u>k</u>t ni<u>h</u>ts; oom; d<u>ee</u>-zuh;
d<u>ee</u> tsyt; **z<u>oh</u>**-v<u>ee</u>-z<u>oh</u>; g<u>e</u>-**shlo**-s<u>e</u>n

3

CONVERSATION

An encounter in the street

TOURISTIN **Entschuldigung! ... ich suche die
Touristeninformation.**
PASSANT **Ja ... die liegt am Theaterplatz.**
TOURISTIN **Und wie komme ich dahin?**
PASSANT **Das ist nicht so leicht ... Moment mal ...
Sie gehen über die Kreuzung, zweite Straße
rechts, über den Marktplatz. Sie sehen
dann die Kirche und das Gasthaus Zur
Rose. Sie nehmen die Straße zwischen
Gasthaus und Kirche, dann ... eins ... zwei
... drei ... ja, dann die vierte Straße rechts,
dann immer geradeaus für etwa
fünfhundert Meter. Sie finden dann sofort
den Theaterplatz.**
TOURISTIN **O, das ist furchtbar schwierig!**
PASSANT **Es macht nichts, die Touristeninformation
ist um diese Zeit sowieso geschlossen.**

3

TOURIST   Excuse me ... I'm looking for the tourist information office.

PASSER-BY   Oh ... that's in Theater Square.

TOURIST   And how do I get there (lit. "come to there")?

PASSER-BY   That's not so easy ... Just a moment ... You go over the crossroads, second street on the right, across the marketplace. You'll then see ("You see then") the church and the Rose Inn. You take the street between the inn and the church ("between inn and church"), then ... one ... two ... three ... yes, then the fourth street on the right, then straight ahead for about five hundred meters. You'll then find ("You find then the") Theater Square immediately.

TOURIST   Oh, that's terribly difficult!

PASSER-BY   It doesn't matter, the information office is closed at this time anyway.

Week 4

- *the indefinite article ("a"/"an") and its negative ("not a"/ "an") and their declensions for the gender and case of the noun*
- *numbers from zero to a million*
- *more on numbers: years and prices*
- *the dative case (used for an indirect object)*
- *some verbs used with indirect objects*

4.1 THE INDEFINITE ARTICLE ("A" / "AN")

4

The word for "a/an" in German is the same as the word for "one": **ein**. When **ein** is used before a noun (e.g., "a cup" or "one cup"), it has the following forms, depending on the gender and case of the noun:

	m.	f.	n.	
	m.	f.	n.	
SU	**ein**	**eine**	**ein**	(nominative)
DO	**einen**	**eine**	**ein**	(accusative)

It has no plural form. Sometimes a plural noun doesn't require an article ("we have friends here"); other times it might be preceded by words such as **einige** (some), **mehrere** (several), or **ein paar** (a few). These words are invariable—they only have one form.

$$\textbf{Wir haben} \left\{ \begin{array}{l} \textbf{Freunde} \\ \textbf{einige Freunde} \\ \textbf{mehrere Freunde} \\ \textbf{ein paar Freunde} \end{array} \right\} \textbf{hier.}$$

The negative of **ein** is **kein**, which means "not a/an/any" or "no...." This does have a plural form (e.g., "no friends").

	singular			plural
	m.	f.	n.	m. f. n.
SU	**kein**	**keine**	**kein**	**keine**
DO	**keinen**	**keine**	**kein**	**keine**

So to say "I don't have any friends" in German, rather than making the verb negative, this would be **Ich habe keine Freunde**. The article **kein** is used constantly, as the following examples show (as this usage is often quite different from English, the phrases in parentheses give the literal meanings):

Wir trinken kein Bier.
We don't drink beer. ("We drink no beer.")
Ich habe keine Ahnung.
I don't have a clue. ("I have no idea.")
Kein Mensch glaubt so etwas.
No one would believe anything like that. ("No person believes such a thing.")
Sie hat Angst, aber er hat keine Angst.
She is afraid but he is not. ("She has fear but he has no fear.")
Er hat keinen Beruf.
He isn't trained for anything. ("He has no profession/trade.")
Wir sind keine Anfänger.
We aren't beginners. ("We are no beginners.")

Note that in German, the indefinite article **ein** is not used when giving someone's profession. And to say what someone doesn't do, **nicht** (not) usually precedes the profession:

Die Mutter ist Lehrerin.
The mother is a teacher.
Er ist nicht Zahnarzt, er ist Kinderarzt.
He's not a dentist, he's a pediatrician.

Also note that the nouns for professions in German usually have a masculine and feminine form:
Lehrer (male teacher), **Lehrerin** (female teacher), **Arzt** (male doctor), **Ärztin** (female doctor).

Exercise 1

Translate the sentences into German.

bauen	to build
die Wohnung (-en)	apartment
das Problem (-e)	problem
installieren	to install
das Wassersystem (-e)	water system
der Strom ("-e)	electricity
der Elektriker (-) /	electrician
die Elektrikerin (-nen)	
die Katastrophe (-n)	catastrophe

4

1 They are buying a house and building apartments [in it].

2 One apartment doesn't have a kitchen.

3 That's a problem, and they are building a kitchen.

4 One apartment doesn't have any water.

5 That's also a problem, but the father is installing a water system.

6 One apartment doesn't have electricity.

7 That's no problem. The son is an electrician.

8 One apartment has a kitchen, water, electricity, and some cupboards, but no windows.

9 That's not a problem, it's a catastrophe.

IMITATED PRONUNCIATION

bow-*e*n; d<u>ee</u> **voh**-noong; dahs prob-**lehm**;
in-stah-**lee**-r*e*n; dahs **vah**-suh-zues-t<u>eh</u>m;
de-uh shtrohm; de-uh*e-**lek**-tri-kuh,
d<u>ee</u>*e-**lek**-tri-k*e*-rin; d<u>ee</u> kah-tahs-**troh**-f*e*

Let's start with the numbers from 0 to 10. **Null** is used mainly when reading decimals or single digits (for example, in telephone numbers).

0	null	6	sechs
1	eins	7	sieben
2	zwei	8	acht
3	drei	9	neun
4	vier	10	zehn
5	fünf		

Let's continue to 20. The first syllable is always stressed.

11 **elf**
12 **zwölf**
13 **dreizehn**
14 **vierzehn**
15 **fünfzehn**
16 **sechzehn** (note that the **-s** of **sechs** is dropped)
17 **siebzehn** (note that the **-en** of **sieben** is dropped)
18 **achtzehn**
19 **neunzehn**
20 **zwanzig**

So far, so good. In the numbers to 30, note how in German the units precede the tens and are joined to them by **und**. The first syllable is always stressed.

21 **einundzwanzig**
22 **zweiundzwanzig**
23 **dreiundzwanzig**
24 **vierundzwanzig**
25 **fünfundzwanzig**
26 **sechsundzwanzig** (because this means "six-and-twenty," the **-s** of **sechs** is included)
27 **siebenundzwanzig** (the **-en** is included)
28 **achtundzwanzig**
29 **neunundzwanzig**
30 **dreißig**

Here are the numbers from 10 to 100 by tens.

10	zehn
20	zwanzig
30	dreißig
40	vierzig
50	fünfzig
60	sechzig (note that the **-s** is dropped)
70	siebzig (the **-en** of **sieben** is dropped)
80	achtzig
90	neunzig
100	hundert

The following examples show how units and tens are combined for the above numbers. For these isolated numbers (as they are not counted in sequence), the stress is always on the second-to-last syllable.

31	einunddreißig
42	zweiundvierzig
53	dreiundfünfzig
64	vierundsechzig
66	sechsundsechzig
75	fünfundsiebzig
77	siebenundsiebzig
86	sechsundachtzig
97	siebenundneunzig

Beyond 100, any number below the millions is written as one word. There is hardly ever an **und** after the hundreds in German (never when numbers are counted in sequence). The units and tens appear in the reverse order from English, with **und** in between.

However long the number, a number spoken in isolation has the stress on the normally stressed syllable of its final component. Long numbers can look intimidating, but it's more manageable if you break them into units:
(300 **drei<u>hund</u>ert**, 507 **fünfhundert<u>sie</u>ben**,
629 **sechshundertneunund<u>zwan</u>zig**)

Practice saying these examples:

101	**hunderteins** (or, less usually) **einhunderteins**
212	**zweihundertzwölf**
323	**dreihundertdreiundzwanzig**
434	**vierhundertvierunddreißig**
545	**fünfhundertfünfundvierzig**
656	**sechshundertsechsundfünfzig**
666	**sechshundertsechsundsechzig**
767	**siebenhundertsiebenundsechzig**
777	**siebenhundertsiebenundsiebzig**
878	**achthundertachtundsiebzig**
989	**neunhundertneunundachtzig**

Here is 100 to 1000 by hundreds:

100	**(ein)hundert**
200	**zweihundert**
300	**dreihundert**
400	**vierhundert**
500	**fünfhundert**
600	**sechshundert**
700	**siebenhundert**
800	**achthundert**
900	**neunhundert**
1000	**tausend**

A million is **eine Million (-en)**, so the figure 5,723,926 would be spoken **fünf Millionen siebenhundertdrei- undzwanzigtausendneunhundertsechsundzwanzig.** A number of more than four figures is separated in thousands by a thin space, not by a comma (e.g., 2 344). Note also (section 4.3) that a comma is used for the decimal point in German (e.g., 3,06).

Years before 2000 are designated, as in English, using only hundreds, so 1992 is **neunzehnhundertzweiund- neunzig**. However, 2005 is **zweitausendfünf**. The 2020s is **die zweitausendzwanziger Jahre**, but note that the 2000s is **die nuller Jahre**.

The ending **-er** is added on to the cardinal number in constructions such as **die zwanziger Jahre** (the '20s). This ending is invariable.

All the numbers can be used with nouns (e.g., **fünfzig Seiten** fifty pages) without any change in the ending. The sole exceptions are numbers ending in **-eins**:

A **Das Buch hat zweihundertundeine Seite.**
(The book has 201 pages.) *or*
B **Das Buch hat zweihundert(und)ein Seiten.**

First, the **-s** in **eins** is dropped before a noun. In A, the **-ein** has the f. sing. ending **-e** with a f. sing. noun. In B, the **-ein** has no ending, the **und** can be dropped, and the noun is plural. Either form is correct.

Cardinal numbers are usually followed by a plural noun, but there are common exceptions, such as units of currency (see section 4.3) and of measurement (see section 8.4).

IMITATED PRONUNCIATION

nool, yns, tsvy, dry, <u>fee</u>-uh, fuenf, zeks, **zee**-ben, ah*k*t, noyn, ts<u>eh</u>n; elf, tsvoelf, **dry**-ts<u>eh</u>n, **fee**-uh-ts<u>eh</u>n, **fuenf**-ts<u>eh</u>n, **zeh**-ts<u>eh</u>n, **zeep**-ts<u>eh</u>n, **ahkt**-ts<u>eh</u>n, **noyn**-ts<u>eh</u>n, **tsvahn**-tsi*h*; **yn***oont-tsvahn-tsi*h*, **tsvy***oont-tsvahn-tsi*h*, ...; **dry**-si*h*, **fee**-uh-tsi*h*, **fuenf**-tsi*h*, **zeh**-tsi*h*, **zeep**-tsi*h*, **ahkt**-tsi*h*, **noyn**-tsi*h*, **hoon**-duht; hoon-duht***yns**; **tow**-z*e*nt; **y**-n*e* mi-li-**y<u>ohn</u>**

4.3 PRICES

The basic unit of German currency is the **Euro** (m.), which is divided into 100 **Cent** (m.). Although often preceded by cardinal numbers, **Euro** and **Cent** are hardly ever found in the plural. Price tags are usually written, and the amounts spoken, as in the following examples.

written	spoken
€0,55	**fünfundfünfzig Cent**
or **55 Cent**	

€1,20	**ein Euro zwanzig**
	eins zwanzig (equally common)
	ein Euro und zwanzig Cent
	(less common)

€4,85	**vier Euro fünfundachtzig**
	vier fünfundachtzig
	vier Euro und fünfundachtzig
	Cent

Price tags are sometimes more explicit, for example:

written	spoken
Kilo €4,80	**vier Euro achtzig das Kilo**
	€4.80 per kilo

Pfd €2,40	**zwei Euro vierzig das Pfund**
	€2.40 per pound
	(the German **Pfund** = 500 grams)

Stück €3,00	**das Stück drei Euro**
Stck €3,00	or **drei Euro das Stück**
	€3.00 for one item / €3.00 each

To ask how much things cost:

Was kostet das?
or **Wie teuer ist das?**
How much is that?

Was kosten die Kartoffeln?
or **Wie teuer sind die Kartoffeln?**
How much are the potatoes?

IMITATED PRONUNCIATION

tsent; **yn**-oy-r<u>oh</u>; dahs keelo; dahs pfoont; dahs shtuek

Exercise 2

1 Ein Buch kostet €12,80 (zwölf Euro achtzig).
Zwei Bücher kosten €25,60 (fünfundzwanzig
Euro sechzig).

Now continue the pattern with the following,
completing the sentences and giving the prices in
figures and words:

2 Ein Brot kostet €2,50 (zwei Euro fünfzig).
Zwei ...

3 Eine Wurst kostet €1,50 (ein Euro fünfzig).
Zwei ...

4 Eine Uhr kostet €85,00 (fünfundachtzig Euro).
Zwei ...

5 Eine Zeitung kostet €1,75 (ein Euro
fünfundsiebzig).
Zwei ...

6 Ein Bett kostet €344,00 (dreihundert
vierundviertzig Euro).
Zwei ...

7 Ein Schrank kostet €505,00 (fünfhundertfünf
Euro).
Zwei ...

8 Ein Messer kostet €3,60 (drei Euro sechzig).
Zwei ...

9 Eine Rose kostet €2,15 (zwei Euro fünfzehn).
Zwei ...

10 Ein Auto kostet €18 000,00 (achtzehntausend
Euro).
Zwei ...

4

4.4 THE DATIVE CASE (INDIRECT OBJECT)

In addition to the nominative case (for the subject) and
the accusative case (for the direct object), there is a
dative case (for an indirect object). In the sentence "I am
lending it to him," "it" is the direct object, while "him" is
the indirect object—typically the recipient of the action.

In English, an indirect object is usually indicated with
"to" or "for":

I am lending it to him.
I am lending it to my friend.
I am lending the book to my friend.

In German, this is indicated with specific case endings for
words related to an indirect object (IO) (including definite
and indefinite articles, pronouns, etc.).

(1) Definite and indefinite articles in the dative case

	singular			plural
	m.	f.	n.	m. f. n.
IO	**dem**	**der**	**dem**	**den**
IO	**(k)einem**	**(k)einer**	**(k)einem**	**keinen**

(2) Indirect object pronouns

singular	plural
mir (to/for) me	**uns** (to/for) us
dir (to/for) you (inf. sing.)	**euch** (to/for) you (inf. pl.)
ihm (to/for) him	**ihnen** (to/for) them
ihr (to/for) her	**Ihnen** (to/for) you (formal)
ihm (to/for) it	

The following table lists the declensions for all three
cases for the definite and indefinite articles:

	singular			plural
	m.	f.	n.	
SU	**der**	**die**	**das**	**die**
	(k)ein	**(k)eine**	**(k)ein**	**keine**

DO	den	die	das	die
	(k)einen	(k)eine	(k)ein	keine
IO	dem	der	dem	den
	(k)einem	(k)einer	(k)einem	keinen

Here are the declensions for the personal pronouns:

SU	DO	IO
ich I	**mich** me	**mir** (to) me
du you (inf. sing.)	**dich** you	**dir** (to) you
er he	**ihn** him	**ihm** (to) him
sie she	**sie** her	**ihr** (to) her
es it	**es** it	**ihm** (to) it
wir we	**uns** us	**uns** (to) us
ihr you (inf. pl.)	**euch** you	**euch** (to) you
sie they	**sie** them	**ihnen** (to) them
Sie you (formal)	**Sie** you	**Ihnen** (to) you

A tip: in the dative (IO) case, the m. and n. singular always ends with **-m**; the f. singular always ends with **-r**; and several of the plural forms end with **-en**.

IMITATED PRONUNCIATION

deh-uh, yn, kyn; d<u>eh</u>n, **y**-n*e*n, **ky**-n*e*n; d<u>eh</u>m, **y**-n*e*m, **ky**-n*e*m; d<u>ee</u>, **y**-n*e*, **ky**-n*e*; deh-uh, **y**-nuh, **ky**-nuh; dahs, yn, kyn; … i*h*, mi*h*, m<u>ee</u>-uh; doo, di*h*, d<u>ee</u>-uh; e-uh, <u>ee</u>n, <u>ee</u>m; z<u>ee</u>, <u>ee</u>-uh; es, <u>ee</u>m; v<u>ee</u>-uh, oons; oy*h*; z<u>ee</u>, <u>ee</u>-n*e*n

4.5 VERBS USED WITH INDIRECT OBJECTS

Some verbs are used with both a direct object and an indirect object:

bringen	to bring (someone something)
geben	to give (someone something)
schenken	to give (someone something) as a present
wünschen	to wish (someone something)

There are also certain verbs in German that require the dative case if the object is human. So, with the following verbs, the person (or pronoun) is an indirect object.

begegnen	to meet (someone)
helfen	to help (someone)
gefallen	to please (someone)
glauben	to believe (someone)
verzeihen	to forgive (someone)
raten	to advise (someone)

IMITATED PRONUNCIATION

bring-en; **geh**-ben; **sheng**-ken; **vuen**-shen; be-**gehg**-nen; **hel**-fen; ge-**fah**-len; **glow**-ben; fuh-**tsy**-en; **rah**-ten

Exercise 3

◀×

Rewrite the following sentences, substituting the nouns in parentheses for those that precede them and making the other changes needed. The words that have to be changed are in *italics*.

Ich bringe *meiner Mutter* (Vater) *eine Zeitung* (Buch).

Ich gebe *sie ihr* (i.e., Buch, Vater) in *der Küche* (Flur).

Ich schenke *meiner Schwester* (Bruder) *eine Katze* (Hund) und wünsche *ihr* einen guten Tag.

VOCABULARY

Read through this new vocabulary used in the following conversation. In the conversation, you'll notice that the present tense is often used to refer to the future.

	heute Abend	this evening
	eingeladen	invited (out)
	man	one
	netten	nice
die	**Dame (-n)**	lady
	rote	red

	bestimmt	definitely
	gut	fine
	Wie viele?	How many?
	sollen	to be supposed to, should
	Ach!	Oh!
	verheiratet	married
	vielleicht	perhaps
	nie	never
	Wieso denn?	Why is that?
	bedeuten	to mean
	gelbe	yellow
die	**Nelke (-n)**	carnation
	Bitte schön!	There you are! You're welcome!
	Viel Spaß!	Have a nice time!

IMITATED PRONUNCIATION

hoy-t*e****ah**-b*e*nt; **yn**-g*e*-<u>lah</u>-d*e*n; mahn; **ne**-t*e*n;
d<u>ee</u> **dah**-m*e*; **<u>roh</u>**-t*e*; b*e*-**shtimt**; goot; v<u>ee</u>-**fee**-l*e*;
zo-l*e*n; ah*k*; fuh-**hy**-<u>rah</u>-t*e*t; <u>fee</u>-**ly**/*t*; n<u>ee</u>;
v<u>ee</u>-**zoh** den; b*e*-**doy**-t*e*n; **gel**-b*e*; d<u>ee</u> **nel**-k*e*;
bi-t*e* sh<u>oen</u>; <u>feel</u> shp<u>ah</u>s

CONVERSATION

A problem of etiquette at the florist's

KUNDE **Ich bin heute Abend eingeladen. Was schenkt man einer netten Dame?**

FLORISTIN **Moment bitte ... Ich helfe Ihnen sofort. Rote Rosen gefallen ihr bestimmt.**

KUNDE **Wie teuer sind rote Rosen?**

FLORISTIN **Sie kosten ein Euro fünfzig das Stück.**

KUNDE **Gut, ich nehme Rosen.**

FLORISTIN **Wie viele sollen es sein? ... fünf ... sieben ... neun ...?**

KUNDE   **Geben Sie mir fünf Stück bitte? ... Ach ja, bringe ich ihrem Mann auch etwas?**

FLORISTIN   **Was!? Die Dame ist verheiratet!!?? Rote Rosen gefallen ihr vielleicht, aber ihr Mann verzeiht Ihnen nie, glauben Sie mir.**

KUNDE   **Wieso denn?**

FLORISTIN   **Rote Rosen bedeuten Liebe. Ich rate Ihnen, schenken Sie ihr gelbe Nelken ... Bitte schön ... Ich wünsche Ihnen viel Spaß heute Abend!**

4

TRANSLATION

CUSTOMER   I've been (lit. "I am") invited out this evening. What does one give a nice lady?

FLORIST   Just a moment, please ... I'll help you right away. Red roses will definitely please her.

CUSTOMER   How much are red roses?

FLORIST   They cost one euro fifty each.

CUSTOMER   Fine, I'll take roses.

FLORIST   How many is it to be ("should it be")? ... five ... seven ... nine?

CUSTOMER   Will you give me five, please? ... Oh yes, shall I take something for her husband too?

FLORIST   What!? The lady is married!!?? Red roses will perhaps please her, but her husband will never forgive you, believe me!

CUSTOMER   Why is that?

FLORIST   Red roses mean love. I'd advise you to give her yellow carnations ... There you are ... Have a lovely evening!

Week 5

- asking questions and making requests
- question words such as "Who?," "When?," "Why?"
- using **nicht** ("not") to make negative sentences
- the imperative (command form)
- adjectives and adverbs
- comparatives and superlatives (e.g., "old," "older," "oldest")

5.1 ASKING QUESTIONS

(1) When the answer is expected to be **ja** (yes) or **nein** (no)

To ask a question with a "yes" or "no" answer, simply begin with the verb, immediately followed by the subject:

Ist er Elektriker?
Is he an electrician?
Kommt er heute?
Is he coming today?
Kommt er oft?
Does he come often?
Hat sie Geschwister?
Does she have (any) brothers and sisters?
Arbeiten sie?
Are they working?

(2) When the answer is expected to be a piece of information

To ask a question requiring particular information in the answer, start with the appropriate question word:

Was?	What?
Wie?	How?
Wo?	Where?
Wer?	Who?
Wen?	Who(m)?
Wem?	To/for whom?
Wann?	When?
Warum?	Why?

The verb follows the question word, with the subject after the verb (except when the subject is the question word itself, as is sometimes the case with **Wer?** and **Was?**, marked with an asterisk below):

Was kosten die Kartoffeln?
What do the potatoes cost?
Was macht das?
How much is that?
*Was kommt jetzt?
What is coming now?
Wie fahren Sie?
How are you traveling? (i.e., by what means)
Wie heißt der Sohn?
What is the son's name? (lit. "How is called the son?")
Wo wohnt die Freundin?
Where does the girlfriend live?
*Wer wohnt hier?
Who lives here? (**wer** indicates a SU)
Wer ist der Besitzer?
Who is the owner?
Wen kennt der Junge?
Who does the boy know? (**wen** indicates a DO)
Wem bringt er die Blumen?
Who is he taking the flowers to? (**wem** indicates an IO)
Wann fahren wir?
When are we traveling? (i.e., when do we leave)

This list of question words is not exhaustive.

IMITATED PRONUNCIATION

ist * e-uh * e-**lek**-tri-kuh; komt * e-uh **hoy**-te; komt * e-uh * oft; haht zee ge-**shvis**-tuh; **ah**-by-ten zee; vahs; vee; voh; ve-uh; vehn; vehm; vahn; vah-**room**; vahs **kos**-ten dee kah-**to**-feln; vahs mahkt dahs; vahs komt yetst; vee **fah**-ren zee; vee hyst deh-uh zohn; voh vohnt dee **froyn**-din; ve-uh vohnt hee-uh; ve-uh * ist deh-uh be-**zit**-suh; vehn kent deh-uh **yoong**-e; vehm bringt * e-uh dee **bloo**-men; vahn **fah**-ren vee-uh

NOTES

(1) If the person you are asking does not know the answer, a typical response might be:

Ich weiß (es) nicht.   I don't know.

The use of **nicht** is explained in section 5.2.

(2) Questions in German are often used to make polite requests. They may use a polite verb form like the English "Would you …?" (see section 12.4) or be in the present tense, which can sound a bit direct in English:

Geben Sie mir bitte die Zeitung?
Will you give me the newspaper, please?
(literally, "Are you giving me the paper, please?")
Reichen Sie mir bitte den Zucker?
Will you pass the sugar, please?

(3) The phrase **Was für (ein)?** means "What sort of (a)?":

Was für ein Auto haben Sie?
What sort of (a) car do you have?
Was für Blumen bringt er?
What sort of flowers does he bring?
Was für einen Teppich sucht sie?
What sort of (a) carpet is she looking for?
Was für ein Mensch ist er?
What sort of a person is he?

In **Was für ein?**, the **ein** has the same ending as in the hypothetical statement on which the question is based:

Sie haben ein Auto. Was für ein Auto haben Sie?
You have a car. What sort of a car do you have?
Sie sucht einen Teppich. Was für einen Teppich sucht sie?
She's looking for a carpet. What sort of a carpet is she looking for?

IMITATED PRONUNCIATION

i*h* vys * es ni*h*t; **geh**-b*e*n z<u>ee</u> m<u>ee</u>-uh **bi**-t*e* d<u>ee</u> **tsy**-toong;
ry-*he*n z<u>ee</u> **bi**-t*e* d*e*hn **tsoo**-kuh; vahs fue-uh * yn *
ow-t<u>oh</u> **hah**-b*e*n z<u>ee</u>; vahs fue-uh **bloo**-m*e*n bringt *
e-uh; vahs fue-uh * **y**-n*e*n **te**-pi*h* z<u>oo</u>kt z<u>ee</u>; vahs fue-uh
* yn mensh * ist * e-uh; z<u>ee</u> **hah**-b*e*n * yn * **ow**-t<u>oh</u>; vahs
fue-uh * yn * **ow**-t<u>oh</u> **hah**-b*e*n z<u>ee</u>; z<u>ee</u> z<u>oo</u>kt * **y**-n*e*n
te-pi*h*; vahs fue-uh * **y**-n*e*n **te**-pi*h* z<u>oo</u>kt z<u>ee</u>

Exercise 1

Insert the correct question word from the column
on the right in the following questions:

1 … für ein Auto hat er?	Wen
2 … kommt er?	Wer
3 … besucht er?	Was
4 … wohnt die Freundin?	Wie
5 … ist sie?	Warum
6 … heißt sie?	Wann
7 … liebt er sie?	Wo

5.2 ■ FORMING NEGATIVE SENTENCES

In section 4.1, we saw how **kein** can be used before a noun to make a sentence negative. But this only works with a noun that can be preceded by an indefinite article (a/an/some/any). Otherwise, **nicht** (not) is used.

Remember that German has strict rules about word order: **nicht** often comes near the end of a sentence. It never comes between the subject and the verb:

Er schwimmt nicht immer. He doesn't always swim.
Wir kennen sie noch nicht. We don't know her yet.
Es funktioniert nicht gut. It isn't working well.

The same principle applies to questions:

Ist er nicht Elektriker? Isn't he an electrician?
Kommt er nicht heute? Isn't he coming today?
Kommt er nicht oft? Doesn't he come often?
Warum arbeiten sie nicht? Why aren't they working?

but
Hat sie keine Geschwister?
Doesn't she have (any) brothers or sisters?

5.3 ■ THE IMPERATIVE (COMMAND FORM)

The formal imperative (the verb form used for requests or commands) is simple: it's just the infinitive (e.g., "to come") followed directly by the pronoun **Sie**:
Kommen Sie sofort! Come at once!

This may sound blunt in English, but it's polite in German and can be further softened by adding **bitte** (please):
Geben Sie mir bitte die Zeitung!
Please give me the paper!

The informal singular (**du** form) is the verb stem plus **-e**, but the **-e** is often dropped in informal usage (and no pronoun is used): **Komm(e)!** Come! **Gib!** Give!

Note that the formal imperative is identical to the formal present tense, so by adding a question mark instead of an exclamation point, the command is turned into a request: **Geben Sie mir bitte die Zeitung?**

However, **sein** (to be) has an irregular imperative:

Seien Sie so nett und bringen Sie mir die Zeitung!
Be so kind and bring me the paper.

VOCABULARY 1

	Bitte schön ...?	Can I help you?
der	**(Stadt)führer (-) /**	(town) guide
die	**(Stadt)führerin (-nen)**	
	fragen	to ask
der	**Chef (-s) /**	boss, manager
die	**Chefin (-nen)**	
	suchen	to look for
	so etwas	such a thing
	sicher	certainly
	drüben	over there
	gucken	to have a look
	(pronounced **koo**-k*e*n)	
	dort	there
	verrückt	crazy
	von	of
	natürlich	of course
	brauchen	to need
	hier	here
	kennen	to know
die	**Stadt (¨e)**	town

IMITATED PRONUNCIATION

bi-t*e* sh<u>oe</u>n; deh-uh **fue**-ruh/-in; deh-uh shtaht-**fue**-ruh/-in, fr<u>ah</u>-gen; deh-uh shef/-in; z<u>oo</u>-k*e*n; z<u>oh</u> * **et**-vahs; **zi**-*h*uh, **drue**-b*e*n; **koo**-k*e*n; doh-uht; fuh-**ruekt**; fon; na-**tue**uh-li*h*; **brow**-*ke*n; h<u>ee</u>-uh, **ke**-n*e*n; d<u>ee</u> shtaht

Exercise 2

Translate this encounter into German, checking any new words in the vocabulary list. Only translate what the speakers say. Compare your translation with the one in the answer key.

A foreign visitor (Fremde) tries to buy a town guide in a bookshop in Bunsenheim

ASSISTANT Can I help you?

VISITOR Hello. Do you have a guide?

ASSISTANT What sort of a guide?

VISITOR A town guide.

ASSISTANT I don't know. Please ask the manager (m.).

VISITOR (to Manager) Hello. I'm looking for a town guide. Do you have such a thing?

MANAGER Yes, certainly. The town guides are over there. Have a look there.

(Ten minutes later)

VISITOR It's crazy. I find town guides of Frankfurt, Gießen, Marburg, and Kassel, but I can't (don't) find a town guide of Bunsenheim.

MANAGER Of course not. Why do we need town guides of Bunsenheim? We live here and know the town!

5.4 ADJECTIVES AND ADVERBS

An adjective is a word that describes a noun. It can either directly precede a noun ("*fine* weather") or follow it after the verb "to be" (**sein**) ("the weather is *fine*").

An adverb is used to describe a verb ("he stumbled *badly*") or other words to give information about manner, time, degree, circumstance, etc. In English, an adverb is often formed by adding -ly, but in German, the same word can be used as either an adjective or adverb:

Das Wetter ist schlecht. The weather is bad.
Das Kind singt schlecht. The child sings badly.

We'll look at adjectives preceding nouns in section 7.3.

Adjectives and adverbs are often preceded by words that qualify them, such as:

sehr	very
zu	too
so	so
ziemlich	fairly, rather, pretty
etwas	rather, somewhat
nicht	not
nicht so	not so
gar nicht	not at all

Der Chef ist gar nicht höflich.
The boss isn't at all polite.
Das Kind trinkt die Milch ziemlich schnell.
The child drinks the milk pretty quickly.

IMITATED PRONUNCIATION

z<u>eh</u>-uh; ts<u>oo</u>; z<u>oh</u>; **ts<u>ee</u>m**-li*h*; **et**-vahs; ni*h*t; ni*h*t z<u>oh</u>; <u>gah</u> ni*h*t

Adjectives and adverbs share the same methods of making comparisons.

(1) Comparatives ("more," "less," etc.)

To make comparatives, add **-er** to the adjective or adverb and, if you need "than," use **als**:

Das Wetter ist heute schlechter als gestern.
The weather is worse today than yesterday.
Das Kind singt schlecht, aber die Mutter singt schlechter.
The child sings badly, but the mother sings worse.

With some adjectives and adverbs, the sound of the vowel changes when the **-er** ending is added:

alt	old	**älter**	older
arm	poor	**ärmer**	poorer

groß	big	**größer**	bigger
hart	hard	**härter**	harder
jung	young	**jünger**	younger
kalt	cold	**kälter**	colder
klug	clever	**klüger**	cleverer
krank	ill	**kränker**	more ill
kurz	short	**kürzer**	shorter
lang	long	**länger**	longer
oft	often	**öfter**	more often
schwach	weak	**schwächer**	weaker
stark	strong	**stärker**	stronger
warm	warm	**wärmer**	warmer

These vowel changes also occur in the superlative.

(2) Superlatives ("most," "least," etc.)

To make superlatives, put **am** before the adjective or adverb and add **-(e)sten** to the word itself:

Das Wetter war vorgestern am schlechtesten.
The weather was worst (of all) the day before yesterday.
Der Vater singt am schlechtesten.
The father sings worst (of all).
Das Wetter war vorvorgestern am schönsten.
The weather was nicest (of all) three days ago (literally: "the day before the day before yesterday").
Die Kusine singt am schönsten.
The cousin (f.) sings the most beautifully (of all).

The ending is usually **-esten** rather than **-sten** when the base word ends in **-s**, **ss**, **-ß** (but not **groß** → **am größten**), **-d**, **-t**, or **-z**.

fies	nasty	**am fiesesten**	nastiest
blass	pale	**am blässesten**	palest
heiß	hot	**am heißesten**	hottest
gesund	healthy	**am gesundesten**	healthiest
hart	hard	**am härtesten**	hardest
schwarz	black	**am schwärzesten**	blackest

However, when a superlative adjective precedes the noun (as in "the finest weather"), **am** is not used, and the ending may be different from **-en** (see section 7.3).

IMITATED PRONUNCIATION

ahlt, **el**-tuh; *ah*m, **eh**-muh; gr<u>oh</u>s, **groe**-suh; haht, **heh**-tuh; yoong, **yueng**-uh; kahlt, **kel**-tuh; kl<u>oo</u>k, **kl<u>ue</u>**-guh; **krahnk**, kreng-kuh; koots, **kuet**-suh; **lahng**, leng-uh; oft, **oef**-tuh; shvah*k*, **shve**-*h*uh; sht*ah*k, **steh**-kuh; v<u>ah</u>m, **veh**-muh

(3) Like English, German has a few adjectives that don't follow the usual pattern:

gut	good	besser	better	am besten	best
viel	much	mehr	more	am meisten	most
hoch	high	höher	higher	am höchsten	highest
nahe	near	näher	nearer	am nächsten	nearest

(4) The construction for "as … as" is **so … wie**

Das Haus ist so klein wie ein Schuppen.
The house is as small as a shed.
Ich komme so schnell wie möglich.
I'll come as quickly as possible.

"just as … as" is **ebenso … wie**:

Das Schlafzimmer ist ebenso groß wie das Wohnzimmer.
The bedroom is just as big as the living room.
Der Vetter singt ebenso schön wie die Kusine.
The male cousin sings just as beautifully as the female cousin.

IMITATED PRONUNCIATION

g<u>oo</u>t, **be**-suh, ahm **bes**-t<u>e</u>n; f<u>ee</u>l, m<u>eh</u>-uh, **ahm** mys-t<u>e</u>n; hoh*k*, **hoe**-uh, ahm **hoe***hs*-t<u>e</u>n; **n**<u>ah</u>-*e*, **n**<u>e</u>-uh, ahm **ne***hs*-t<u>e</u>n; z<u>oh</u> … v<u>ee</u>; **eh**-b<u>e</u>n-z<u>oh</u> … v<u>ee</u>

Exercise 3

1 Meine Mutter ist alt, aber mein Vater ist älter.
Complete the following sentences in the same way.

2 Mein Bruder ist groß, aber meine Schwester ist …

3 Die Frau ist jung, aber die Wirtin ist …

4 Der Sohn ist klug, aber die Tochter ist …

5 Das Zimmer ist warm, aber das Bett ist …

6 Die gelbe Nelke ist lang, aber die rote Rose ist …

7 Die Frau ist nett, aber der Mann ist …

5

VOCABULARY 2

Read through these new words that are used in the conversation that follows:

der	**Hausbesitzer (-) /**	houseowner
	die Hausbesitzerin (-nen)	
	dieser/diese/dieses	this (m./f./n.)
das	**Wohnzimmer (-)**	living room
das	**Schlafzimmer (-)**	bedroom
der	**Mieter (-) /**	tenant
	die Mieterin (-nen)	
der	**Flur (-e)**	hall
	dunk(e)l*	dark
die	**Straße (-n)**	street
	laut	noisy
	eigentlich	really, actually
	oben	upstairs
	hell	light, bright

der	Raum (¨e)	room, space
	bestimmt	definitely
	breit	wide
	unten	downstairs
die	Decke (-n)	ceiling
	niedrig	low
	winzig	tiny
	gegenüber	opposite
die	Aussicht (-en)	view
	wunderschön	glorious, splendid
der	Garten (¨)	garden
	liegen	to lie (be horizontal)
	nämlich	after all, in fact
	hinten	at the back, rear
	ruhig	quiet
	vorn	at the front
	nehmen	to take
	übrigens	by the way
der	Monat (-e)	month
	teu(e)r*	expensive
	jetzt	now, at present
	zahlen	to pay

* The letter in parentheses disappears when another syllable such as **-er** is added to the adjective/adverb.

IMITATED PRONUNCIATION

d*ee* **hows**-b*e*-zit-s*e*/-rin; d*ees*; dahs **vohn**-tsi-muh; dahs **shlahf**-tsi-muh; deh-uh **mee**-tuh/-rin; deh-uh **floo**-uh; **doong**-k*e*l; d*ee* **shtrah**-s*e*; lowt; **y**-g*e*nt-li*h*; **oh**-b*e*n; hel; deh-uh rowm; b*e*-**shtimt**; bryt; **oon**-t*e*n; d*ee* **de**-k*e*; **nee**-dri*h*; **win**-tsi*h*; **geh**-gen***ue**-buh; d*ee* **ows**-zi*h*t; **voon**-duh-shoen; deh-uh **gah**-ten; **lee**-g*e*n; **nem**-li*h*; **hin**-ten; **roo**-i*h*; fohn; **neh**-m*e*n; **ueb**-ri-g*e*ns; deh-uh **moh**-naht; **toy**-uh; yetst; **tsah**-l*e*n

A homeowner shows three vacant apartments to a prospective tenant

In the ground-floor apartment:

HAUSBESITZERIN	**Diese Wohnung ist schön groß, zwei Wohnzimmer, vier Schlafzimmer, zwei Toiletten ...**
MIETER	**Der Flur ist zu dunkel, und die Straße ist ziemlich laut. Diese Wohnung ist mir eigentlich zu groß. Ich brauche keine vier Schlafzimmer, eigentlich nur zwei ... Sind die Wohnungen oben kleiner?**
HAUSBESITZERIN	**Ja. Sie sind auch etwas heller als diese.**

In the first-floor apartment at the front:

HAUSBESITZERIN	**Diese Räume gefallen Ihnen bestimmt ... nur ein Wohnzimmer, aber breiter und länger als das Wohnzimmer unten.**
MIETER	**Ja, schön, aber die Decke ist niedriger als unten. Die drei Schlafzimmer sind mir zu winzig, und es ist ebenso laut hier wie unten.**

In the first-floor apartment at the rear:

HAUSBESITZERIN	**Diese Wohnung ist am schönsten. Hier sind nur zwei Schlafzimmer. Sie sind aber etwas größer als die Schlafzimmer gegenüber. Die Aussicht ist wunderschön, der Garten liegt nämlich hinten.**
MIETER	**Ja, und diese Wohnung ist auch viel ruhiger als die Wohnungen vorn. Ja, ich nehme sie ... Wie hoch ist übrigens die Miete?**

HAUSBESITZERIN **Neunhundertfünfzig Euro pro Monat.**
MIETER **Was!!?? Nein, das ist mir zu teuer.**
Das ist viel mehr, als ich jetzt zahle.

TRANSLATION

In the ground-floor apartment:

HOUSEOWNER This apartment is beautifully spacious, two living rooms, four bedrooms, two toilets …

TENANT The hall is too dark, and the street is rather noisy. This apartment is really too large for me. I don't need four bedrooms, really only two … Are the apartments upstairs smaller?

HOUSEOWNER Yes. They're somewhat lighter than this one, too.

In the first-floor apartment at the front:

HOUSEOWNER You'll definitely like these rooms … only one living room, but it's wider and longer than the living room downstairs.

TENANT Yes, nice, but the ceiling is lower than downstairs. The three bedrooms are too tiny for me, and it's just as noisy here as downstairs.

In the first-floor apartment at the rear:

HOUSEOWNER This apartment is the nicest of all. Here there are only two bedrooms. But they're somewhat larger than the bedrooms opposite. The view is glorious. The garden's at the back, after all.

TENANT Yes, and this apartment is quieter than the apartments at the front too. Yes, I'll take it … By the way, how much is the rent?

HOUSEOWNER Nine hundred fifty euros a month.

TENANT What!!?? No, that's too expensive for me. That's much more than I'm paying now.

Week 6

- prepositions ("in," "by," "of," etc.)
- how prepositions affect the case of the following noun or pronoun
- the expression **es gibt** ("there is"/"there are")

6.1 PREPOSITIONS

Prepositions are words or groups of words that usually precede a noun or pronoun (hence the name "preposition") to indicate its relationship with other words in the sentence. They can show information such as direction, time, location, agent, spatial relationship, etc.:

going *into* the house
stolen *by* a thief
a letter *from* you
fond *of* her mother
insist *on* payment

Because different prepositions can indicate different functions of the following noun or pronoun, this has an impact on the grammatical case. The nouns following some prepositions are direct objects, so take the accusative; some are indirect objects, so take the dative; and some take either, depending on the meaning.

The most common German prepositions are listed below, grouped according to the case(s) they require. Although the primary translations are shown, note that the meaning of prepositions depends on context. You'll become familiar with how they are used as you come across them in various situations.

(1) Prepositions followed by a DO (accusative case)

durch	through, by, by means of
für	for
gegen	against, toward
ohne	without
um	around, at (time of day)

Note these three contracted forms that are frequently found when followed by **das**:

durchs (= durch das) Fenster through the window
fürs (= für das) Theater for the theater
ums (= um das) Feuer around the fire

(2) Prepositions followed by an IO (dative case)

aus out of, from

bei with, at (so-and-so's house), near, in (such-and-such conditions or weather), during, in the process/course of

mit with

nach to (certain locations, including one's own house: **nach Hause**), after (time), according to

seit since, for (period of time up to now)

von from (place and time), by (indicating agency or authorship), of (possession)

zu to (certain locations), at (e.g., at home: **zu Hause**)

Note these contracted forms when followed by **dem**:

beim (= bei dem) Gewitter in/during the thunderstorm
vom (= von dem) Dach from the roof
zum (= zu dem) Arzt to the doctor

and when followed by **der** (f. sing. IO):

zur (= zu der) Seite to the side, aside

(3) Prepositions followed by either a DO or an IO

If the context indicates a change of location or condition, these prepositions are followed by a DO (accusative); otherwise they are followed by an IO (dative).

	DO	IO
an	on to (the side of); up to (the edge of)	at, by, on (the side of a nonhorizontal surface); on (with days and dates)
auf	on to (the top of a horizontal surface)	on (the top of a horizontal surface)
hinter	(to) behind	behind
in	into	in (spatial and temporal, though with years need **im Jahre**, e.g., **im Jahre 2022**); inside, within
neben	(to) next to, (to) alongside	next to, alongside, along with
über	across, over (i.e., from one side to the other), via	above, over (i.e., on top of)
unter	(to) underneath, (to) below, under (from one side to the other)	below, underneath, under
vor	(to) in front of, (to) before	in front of, before; (in past time contexts) ago
zwischen	(to) in between	between

6

Note these contracted forms when follwed by **das**:

ans (= an das) Feuer　　　up to the fire
aufs (= auf das) Wasser　　onto the water
ins (= in das) Netz　　　　into the net
vors (= vor das) Auto　　　in front of the car

and when followed by **dem**:

am (= an dem) Montag　　　on Monday
im (= in dem) Schnee　　　in the snow

The following sentences illustrate the principle underlying the different meanings conveyed by a DO or IO:

Kai geht an den Schrank, Lena steht am Schrank.
Kai goes to the wardrobe. Lena stands by the wardrobe.
Er legt die Zeitung auf den Tisch, sie liegt jetzt auf dem Tisch.
He puts (lays) the newspaper on the table. It's now (lying) on the table.
Kai springt hinter den Stuhl, Lena ist schon hinter dem Stuhl.
Kai jumps behind the chair. Lena is already behind the chair.
Kai geht jetzt in den Garten, Lena singt im Garten.
Kai now goes into the garden. Lena is singing in the garden.
Die Katze geht neben den Stuhl, der Hund liegt schon neben dem Stuhl.
The cat goes next to the chair. The dog is already lying next to the chair.
Die Katze springt über den Tisch, die Uhr hängt über dem Tisch.
The cat jumps over the table. The clock is hanging above the table.
Der Hund kriecht unter den Tisch, die Zeitung liegt unter dem Tisch.
The dog creeps under the table. The newspaper is (lies) under the table.

6

(4) The preposition **bis** can be used in two ways

When expressing time/numbers, it means "until," "up to," "by" and is followed by a DO (accusative case):

bis nächstes Jahr until next year
bis nächsten Montag until next Monday

In other expressions, it means "up to," "as far as." In this usage, **bis** cannot stand alone, except before place names. It must be followed by another preposition, such as **an**, **auf**, or **in**. The case of the noun or pronoun is determined by this second preposition.

The following example shows both usages:

Oskar kommt nur bis Bunsenheim, findet ein Gasthaus, geht bis an die Tür, wartet bis fünf Uhr, zählt bis fünfzig, kommt dann bis in die Gaststube, aber: keiner ist da!
Oskar only gets as far as Bunsenheim, finds an inn, goes up to the door, waits until five o'clock, counts up to fifty, then gets as far as the lounge, but—no one is there!

(5) The preposition **gegenüber** means "opposite," "toward," "compared to"

The position of **gegenüber** is similar to English usage. The nouns it relates to are IOs (dative case):

Die Kirche steht am Marktplatz gegenüber dem Gasthaus Zur Rose, und Sie finden das Theater am Theaterplatz gegenüber der Touristeninformation.
The church is on the marketplace opposite the Rose Inn, and you'll find the theater on Theater Square opposite the tourist information office.

6

VOCABULARY 1

Read through these new words before you do the
following exercises. We've stopped including the
imitated pronunciation, as you should be getting
familiar with this now, but keep listening to the audio!

der	Verbrecher (-) /	criminal
	die Verbrecherin (-nen)	
der	Pinsel (-)	paintbrush
die	Palette (-n)	palette
die	Hand (¨e)	hand
das	Bild (-er)	picture
die	Sache (-n)	thing
die	Tischdecke (-n)	tablecloth
das	Brot (-e)	loaf of bread
das	Glas (¨er)	glass
die	Flasche (-n)	bottle
der	Korken (-)	cork
das	Etikett (-en)	label
	wichtig	important
die	Feile (-n)	file
der	Einbrecher (-) /	burglar, intruder
	die Einbrecherin (-nen)	
die	Haustür (-en)	front door
	klopfen	to knock
	niemand, keiner	no one
	gucken	to peep
	finden	to find
das	Nummernschild (-er)	number plate, license plate
die	Garage (-n)	garage
	zurück	back
	stecken	to put (inside or between)
der	Rahmen (-)	frame
	öffnen	to open
die	Treppe (-n)	stairs (i.e., staircase)
	sitzen	to sit
das	Skelett (-e)	skeleton
die	Axt (¨e)	ax

Exercise 1

The story that follows describes a prisoner painting a picture of objects on a table. On the tablecloth is a loaf of bread cut open to reveal a file that has been inserted into it. Next to the loaf is a glass of wine and behind it, a wine bottle. Complete the story by inserting prepositions in the gaps marked (P) and putting the right case endings on the articles **d-** and **ein-**. Here are the prepositions, listed in the order they are required:

mit, in, vor, auf, auf, neben, hinter, mit, auf, für, in

Der Verbrecher steht (P) ein- Pinsel und ein- Palette (P) d- Hand (P) ein- Bild. (P) d- Bild sind mehrere Sachen. (P) ein- Tischdecke liegt ein Brot. (P) d- Brot ist ein Glas, und (P) d- Brot ist eine Flasche (P) ein- Korken. (P) d- Flasche ist ein Etikett. Was ist aber (P) d- Verbrecher am wichtigsten? Die Feile (P) d- Brot natürlich!

6

Exercise 2

Translate the following sentences into German, using the vocabulary list on the opposite page. The appropriate prepositions are indicated at the end of each sentence. (The English words in parentheses are just there to help with the meaning; you don't have to translate them.)

The intruder goes up to the front door. (**bis an**)

He knocks on the door. (**an**)

No one comes to the door. (**zu**)

He goes around the house and peeps through the windows. (**um**, **durch**)

He finds a car without (a) license plate between the house and the garage. (**ohne**, **zwischen**)

He goes back to the front door. (**an**)

He pushes a file between the door and the frame. (**zwischen**)

He opens the door with the file and goes into the hall. (**mit**, **in**)

Opposite him on the stairs sits a skeleton with an ax in its ("the") hand! (**gegenüber**, **auf**, **mit**, **in**)

6.2 THE EXPRESSION **ES GIBT** ("THERE IS," "THERE ARE")

To express the idea that something exists (or not) or is available (or not), we use "there is/are" in English. In this frequently used expression, the verb conjugates according to whether what's being talked about is singular or plural or whether the time frame is the present, past, future, etc.:

There is a mouse in the kitchen.
There are foxes by the river.
There was cake at the party.
There will be pizza for lunch.

In German, the equivalent of "there is/are" is **es gibt** (from **geben**, "to give": note that in this irregular verb, the vowel in the verb stem changes in this third-person singular form). In this impersonal expression, **es** (it) is the subject, so what is being talked about is a DO (requiring the accusative case):

Es gibt heute einen Film im Fernsehen.
There's a film on television today.
Gibt es keinen Kuchen mehr?
Is there no more cake?
Es gibt mehrere Fehler in dem Brief.
There are several mistakes in the letter.
Es gibt einige Ausländer im Hotel.
There are some foreigners at the hotel.
Es gibt jetzt Abendbrot!
Now we're going to have dinner! ("There is dinner now.")

As you see in these examples, **es gibt** is used for both singular and plural.

The question **Was gibt es?** (usually spoken **Was gibt's?**) means "What is there?" (e.g., for a meal, available in a shop, on television, etc.).

VOCABULARY 2

der	Hotelgast (¨e)	hotel guest
das	Fernsehen	television
	im Fernsehen	on television
	heute Abend	this evening
der	Kellner (-) /	waiter/waitress
	die Kellnerin (-nen)	
die	Fernsehzeitung (-en)	TV magazine
die	Woche (-n)	week
	diese Woche	this week
die	Tageszeitung (-en)	daily newspaper
	hier	here
	leider	unfortunately
	gestern	yesterday

Exercise 3

6

Translate the following short conversation into German, using the words in the vocabulary list above.

In the lounge of a hotel

HOTEL GUEST What is there on television this evening?

WAITER I don't know.

HOTEL GUEST Look in the TV magazine, please.
(**in** + DO)

WAITER There is no TV magazine this week.

HOTEL GUEST Is there a daily paper?

WAITER Yes, here is a daily paper ... but
unfortunately it is from yesterday. (**von**)

Week 7

- words with the same declensions as **der, die, das**, including the demonstrative pronouns "this" and "that"
- the possessive adjectives "my," "your," etc. (which have the same declensions as **ein**)
- endings added to adjectives when they precede a noun
- ordinal numbers ("first," "second," etc.) and fractions
- the informal **du** for addressing someone you're on familiar terms with
- word order in a simple German sentence

7.1 WORDS WITH THE SAME DECLENSIONS AS DER, DIE, DAS

There are six other words that decline in the same way as **der, die, das**, as they qualify the following noun in a similar way. This means their ending depends on the gender, number, and case of the noun.

The stem for each word is listed below: see the table on the next page for the endings in each context.

dies-	this, these (*sometimes* that, those)
jed-	each, every, any
welch- ?/!	which?, what?, what (a)!
jen-	that, those
solch-	such
manch-	quite a few, a fair number of

(1) The usual way to say "that" is **der, die,** or **das** spoken with emphasis, or **dies-**. The pronoun **jen-** is not used often, unless paired with **dies-**: for example, in the expression **jen- , dies-** (the former, the latter).

(2) In the singular, **solch-** and **manch-** have the alternatives **solch ein** and **manch ein**: in that case, only the **ein** takes endings. To convey the meaning of **solch ein**, there is also the option **ein solch-** (endings as in section 7.3) and the frequently used **so ein**.

(3) manch- has no exact equivalent in English. It means more than "some" and fewer than "many." Whether singular or plural in form, it is plural in meaning.

Here is a summary of the different endings, using **dies-** as a model:

	singular			plural
	m.	f.	n.	m. f. n.
SU	dieser	diese	dieses*	diese
DO	diesen	diese	dieses*	diese
IO	diesem	dieser	diesem	diesen

*The neuter ending **-as** in **das** is replaced by **-es** in all six of these words.

And here are some examples in context:

dies-   **Kennen Sie dieses Buch aus der Hugo-Reihe?**
Do you know this book from the Hugo series?

jed-   **Jedes Kind bekommt ein Ei.**
Each/every child will get an egg.
Ich bin für jeden Vorschlag offen.
I am open to any suggestion.

welch- ?/!   **Auf welchen Bus warten Sie?**
Which bus are you waiting for?
Welchen Druck hat der Reifen?
What pressure does the tire have?

jen-   **Der Film stammt aus jener Zeit vor dem 1. Weltkrieg.**
The film comes from that period before World War I.
Wir sprechen oft über dieses und jenes.
We often talk about this and that.

solch-	**Er hat solche Schwierigkeiten mit seinem Vater.**
	He has such difficulties with his father.
	Wir haben solches Glück mit dem Wetter.
	We're having such luck with the weather.
manch-	**Mancher Polizist fährt selbst zu schnell.**
	Quite a few policemen drive too fast themselves.

All six of these words can also be used on their own, with a noun being understood from the context:

Ich trinke aus diesem Glas. Trinken Sie aus diesem?
I'll drink from this glass. Will you drink from this one? (indicating the glass)

jeder (DO **jeden**, IO **jedem**) on its own means "everyone," just as **keiner** (DO **keinen**, IO **keinem**) on its own means "no one," "nobody."

7.2 POSSESSIVE ADJECTIVES

The possessive adjectives ("my," "your," "his," "her," etc.) decline following the pattern of the indefinite article **ein**. When they are used with a masculine singular noun that is the subject (nominative case), they are:

mein my
dein your (informal sing.)
sein his
ihr her
sein its
unser our
euer your (informal pl.)
ihr their
Ihr your (formal: sing. & pl.)

An important thing to keep in mind is that the form of the possessive adjective needs to agree with the gender, number, and case of the noun it precedes—i.e., what is <u>possessed</u>: for example, **unser Freund** (m.), but **unsere Freundin** (f.) (in the nominative case).

Below are the different endings of the possessive adjectives, using **unser** and **Ihr** as examples:

	singular			plural
	m.	f.	n.	m. f. n.
SU	**unser**	**unsere**	**unser**	**unsere**
DO	**unseren**	**unsere**	**unser**	**unsere**
IO	**unserem**	**unserer**	**unserem**	**unseren**

(Don't mistake the **-er** in the stem of **unser** for a declension ending: here, it's part of the word!)

	singular			plural
	m.	f.	n.	m. f. n.
SU	**Ihr**	**Ihre**	**Ihr**	**Ihre**
DO	**Ihren**	**Ihre**	**Ihr**	**Ihre**
IO	**Ihrem**	**Ihrer**	**Ihrem**	**Ihren**

All these possessive adjectives can also be used on their own (without a noun) as possessive pronouns meaning "mine, yours, his, hers, its, ours, theirs."

The endings are the same as in the tables above, except that when used as a pronoun, the masculine singular nominative (SU) adds **-er**, and the neuter singular nominative (SU) and accusative (DO) add **-s**:

Leihen Sie mir bitte Ihren Bleistift. Meiner ist weg.
Lend me your pencil, please. Mine has disappeared (literally: "is away").
Mein Fahrrad ist fünf Jahre alt. Wie alt ist Ihrs?
My bicycle is five years old. How old is yours?

Exercise 1

1 Geht er ohne seine Freundin ins Theater?
  Nein, er geht mit seiner Freundin ins Theater.

Complete the following sentences in the same way.

2 Ist sie ohne ihre Schwester bei Müllers eingeladen?
  Nein, ...

3 Kommt der Vater mit unserem Geschenk für
  die Mutter?
  Nein, ...

4 Esse ich den Kuchen ohne eine Tasse Kaffee?
  Nein, ...

5 Geht er ohne seinen Stadtführer durch Frankfurt?
  Nein, ...

6 Mache ich das Abendbrot mit meiner Tochter?
  Nein, ...

7 Geht sie mit ihrem Bruder zur Tante?
  Nein, ...

8 Kaufen wir die Wurst mit einer Cola?
  Nein, ...

7.3 ADJECTIVES BEFORE NOUNS

As we've seen, predicate adjectives (used after a verb such as **sein**) do not decline (see section 5.4). However, attributive adjectives (which directly precede the noun) do change form.

Which endings they take depends on two things: (a) the gender, number, and case of the noun they modify; and (b) whether they are preceded by an article or not. The following three rules deal with (b).

(1) Adjectives after a definite article, demonstrative, or the other words in section 7.1 (**der**, **dieser**, etc.)

If the article unequivocally shows the gender and case of the noun, the adjective simply takes an **-en** or **-e** ending.

	singular			plural
	m.	f.	n.	m. f. n.
SU	der arme Mann	die arme Frau	das arme Kind	die armen Leute
DO	den armen Mann	die arme Frau	das arme Kind	die armen Leute
IO	dem armen Mann	der armen Frau	dem armen Kind	den armen Leuten*

*Plural nouns in the dative (IO) case always have **-n** added to the plural form unless the plural already ends in **-n** or is a plural loanword, such as **Autos**.

Here is a summary of the endings:

	singular			plural
	m.	f.	n.	m. f. n.
SU	-e	-e	-e	-en
DO	-en	-e	-e	-en
IO	-en	-en	-en	-en

(2) Adjectives after an indefinite article or possessive adjective (**ein**, **kein**, **mein**, etc.)

These adjectives decline just like those preceded by a definite article. The only exceptions are the nominative (SU) singular (m., f., n.) and the accusative (DO) singular (f., n.): in these cases, it takes the same endings as the definite article (**de̲r**, **di̲e̲**, **da̲s̲**):

	singular			plural
	m.	f.	n.	m. f. n.
SU	ihr armer Mann	seine arme Frau	ihr armes Kind	ihre armen Kinder
DO	ihren armen Mann	seine arme Frau	ihr armes Kind	ihre armen Kinder
IO	ihrem armen Mann	seiner armen Frau	ihrem armen Kind	ihren armen Kindern

Here is a summary of the endings:

	singular			plural
	m.	f.	n.	m. f. n.
SU	-er	-e	-es	-en
DO	-en	-e	-es	-en
IO	-en	-en	-en	-en

(3) Unpreceded adjectives

In cases where no article, demonstrative, possessive, etc., is used, the adjective must decline like the definite article (see section 7.1):

	singular			plural
	m.	f.	n.	m. f. n.
SU	**kalter Wein**	**kalte Limonade**	**kaltes Bier**	**kalte Getränke**
DO	**kalten Wein**	**kalte Limonade**	**kaltes Bier**	**kalte Getränke**
IO	**kaltem Wein**	**kalter Limonade**	**kaltem Bier**	**kalten Getränken**

Here is a summary of the endings for unpreceded adjectives:

	singular			plural
	m.	f.	n.	m. f. n.
SU	-er	-e	-es	-e
DO	-en	-e	-es	-e
IO	-em	-er	-em	-en

The principle behind the adjective endings for contexts (2) and (3) is that the adjective needs to carry the marker for case and gender if the preceding word does not. So, in context (2), **ein** does not show the **-r** ending in the m. sing. (SU) or the **-s** in the n. sing. (SU/DO). Thus the adjective adds them. In (3), there is no preceding article, so the adjective has to take the endings (except that the n. sing. **das** [SU/DO] becomes **-es** [see section 7.1]).

7.4 ORDINAL NUMBERS AND FRACTIONS

(1) The ordinal numbers ("first," "second," "third," etc.) are formed as follows:

• 1st: **erst**.

• 2nd to 19th:
Add a **-t** to the cardinal number (section 4.2): **zweit** (second), **neunt** (ninth), **achtzehnt** (eighteenth), etc.

Exceptions:
3rd	**dritt**	(**-ei-** becomes **-i-**)
7th	**siebt**	(**sieben** loses the **-en**)
8th	**acht**	(**acht** does not add another **-t**)

• 20th onward:
Add **-st** to the cardinal number: **fünfunddreißigst** (thirty-fifth), **hundertst** (hundredth), and **tausendst** (thousandth).

Ordinal numbers are mostly used as adjectives before nouns, so they take the endings described in section 7.3:

Die fünfte Person von rechts ist mein Vater.
The fifth person from the right is my father.
Ich nehme gern ein zweites Glas von dem herrlichen Wein.
I'd love a second glass of that wonderful wine.

The following examples use the same endings as in section 7.3 context (3):
Sie benutzen als Erster (or **Erste** if person spoken to is female) **unsere neue Maschine.**
You're the first to use our new machine.
Ich bin als Siebter mit der Prüfung fertig.
I'm the seventh to finish the test.

(2) Apart from **die Hälfte (-n)** (half), fractions are formed by adding **-el** to the ordinal number, which then becomes a neuter noun: for example, **das Viertel (-)** (quarter),

das Zehntel (-) (tenth). Or to give both parts of a fraction: **zwei Drittel** (two-thirds), **drei Achtel** (three-eighths), etc.

To say "half (of) the ..." is often **die Hälfte von** ... (or, instead of **von**, the genitive case, see section 10.1):

Die Hälfte von dem Geld gehört mir.
Half of the money belongs to me.

However, when "half" is followed by "a/an," the adjective **halb** is used: **eine halbe Stunde** (half an hour), **ein halbes Brot** (half a loaf of bread).

"One and a half" is **anderthalb, eineinhalb**, or even **einundeinhalb**, and "five and a half" is **fünfeinhalb** or **fünfundeinhalb**. These do not take any adjective endings even when they precede nouns.

Many compound words contain **Viertel**, such as **eine Viertelstunde** (a quarter of an hour); **ein Viertelliter** (a quarter of a liter) (m. or n., no change in the plural).

7.5 INFORMAL ADDRESS

As we've seen, there are several ways to say "you" in German. In the examples so far, we've focused on the formal **Sie**, which is the form to use if you don't know someone well or a level of courtesy is required.

But for people you're on more casual, familiar terms with—family, friends, classmates, etc.—the informal second person is used. In the singular, this is **du** (you), **dein** (your) (nominative), and their declensions. The **du** form of regular verbs in the present tense is the stem + **(e)st**. (The **e** is added after stems ending in **-t** or **-d**.)

In the plural (when speaking to more than one person), use **ihr** (you), **euer** (your) nominative, and their declensions. The verb form is the stem + **(e)t**.

7.6 WORD ORDER

A key rule in German is that the verb has to be the second element in a sentence. This is the case whether it starts with a subject or some other element:

location	verb	subject
Auf dem Bild	**sind**	**mehrere Sachen.**
Auf einer Tischdecke	**liegt**	**ein Brot.**
Neben dem Brot	**ist**	**ein Glas.**
Hinter dem Brot	**ist**	**eine Flasche mit einem Korken.**
Auf der Flasche	**ist**	**ein Etikett.**

In simple statements like this, while the equivalent in English would often start with the subject, the German order is also possible: "In the picture are several objects." "On the tablecloth is a loaf of bread." "Next to the bread is a glass." "Behind the bread is a bottle with a cork." etc.

However, in German, other information might be at the beginning of a statement, such as a direct or indirect object, if this has been previously mentioned. But no matter what comes first, the verb must come second.

Here are some examples:

DO	verb	subject	rest
zwei Cola	**wollen**	**Sie**	**aber nur eine Wurst**
den Theaterplatz	**finden**	**Sie**	**dann sofort**
so etwas	**glaubt**	**kein Mensch**	
viel Spaß	**wünsche**	**ich**	**Ihnen heute Abend**
einen Stadtführer	**suche**	**ich**	

IO	verb	subject	rest
ihr	**gefallen**	**rote Rosen**	**bestimmt**
Ihnen	**wünsche**	**ich**	**viel Spaß heute Abend**

Exercise 2

Put the correct word from the column on the right into the following sentences. There may be more than one grammatically correct possibility, but not all of them make sense.

1 … glaubt einem Verbrecher.	Solches
2 … Blumen sind für die Freundin?	Keiner
3 … Kuchen haben sie für das Kind.	Welches?/!
4 … Mann finde ich nett.	Jeder
5 … Wein schmeckt wunderbar.	Dieser
6 … Glück haben wir mit dem Wetter.	Welche?/!
7 … Buch aus der Hugo-Reihe kennen Sie?	Jede
8 … Hausbesitzer hat Schwierigkeiten.	Keinen
9 … Katze kommt ins Haus./?	Diesen

7

VOCABULARY

	einkaufen	to do the shopping
	Jawohl!	Yes, certainly!
die	**Einkaufsliste (-n)**	shopping list
	alles	everything
	erst	first (of all)
	holen	to fetch, to go and get
der	**Bäcker (-) /**	baker
	die Bäckerin (-nen)	
das	**Weißbrot (-e)**	loaf of white bread
	frisch	fresh
das	**Brötchen (-)**	roll
	billig	cheap
der	**Supermarkt**	supermarket
	fahren	to drive, to go (by means of transportation)
	heute Nachmittag	this afternoon
	dorthin	(to) there
	Na gut!	All right then!

der	**Metzger (-)** /	butcher
die	**Metzgerin (-nen)**	
	halb	half
das	**Pfund (-e)**	pound (500 grams)
	(-) after numbers	
das	**Hackfleisch**	ground meat
	gekocht	boiled
der	**Schinken**	ham
	bedienen	to serve
	man	one, they, people
	immer	always
das	**Fleisch**	meat
	lieber	rather
die	**Altstadt**	old town
	müssen	to have to, must
	dahin	(to) there
das	**Gemüsegeschäft**	produce stand
der	**Kopfsalat (-e)**	lettuce
	fest	firm
die	**Gurke (-n)**	cucumber
die	**Bohne (-n)**	bean
	grüne Bohnen	French beans, green beans
die	**Sache (-n)**	thing, item
der	**Salat (-e)**	salad
	ander-	other
das	**Gemüse**	vegetables
	eilen	to be urgent
	doch	after all
der	**Markt (¨e)**	market
	unbedingt	definitely
das	**Ei (-er)**	egg
	noch	still
	viele	many, a lot
	kriegen	to get

7

Translate this conversation into English. You'll find the vocabulary you need on pp.86–87.

Putting off the shopping

SIE **Gehst du bitte jetzt einkaufen?**

ER **Jawohl! Hast du eine Einkaufsliste für mich?**

SIE **Nein, ich sage dir alles ... Erst hol bitte vom Bäcker ein kleines Weißbrot und zehn frische Brötchen.**

ER **Sie sind billiger im Supermarkt, und wir fahren heute Nachmittag dorthin.**

SIE **Na gut! Dann kauf beim Metzger ein halbes Pfund Hackfleisch und dreihundertfünfzig Gramm gekochten Schinken.**

ER **Beim Metzger bedient man mich immer schlecht. Ich kaufe Fleisch lieber in der Altstadt, und heute Nachmittag müssen wir auch dahin.**

SIE **Na gut! Vom Gemüsegeschäft brauche ich dann einen Kopfsalat, anderthalb Pfund kleine feste Tomaten, eine schöne Gurke, zehn Pfund Kartoffeln und ein Pfund grüne Bohnen.**

ER **Die Sachen für den Salat und das andere Gemüse eilen nicht, und morgen ist doch Markt.**

SIE **Na gut, aber ich brauche unbedingt Eier.**

ER **Nein, brauchst du nicht. Wir haben noch viele. Eier kriegen wir dann auch vom Markt.**

SIE **Na gut, dann brauchst du nicht einkaufen gehen.**

7

Exercise 3

Practice repeating the conversation from memory, using the following key words as a guide.

SIE einkaufen?
ER   Einkaufsliste?
SIE sage alles … Bäcker …Weißbrot … Brötchen
ER   in den Supermarkt fahren
SIE Metzger … Hackfleisch … Schinken
ER   schlecht … Altstadt … Nachmittag
SIE Gemüsegeschäft … Kopfsalat … Tomaten …
     Gurke … Kartoffeln … Bohnen
ER   eilen nicht … Markt
SIE Eier
ER   brauchst nicht … noch viele … Markt
SIE nicht einkaufen

Exercise 4

Now, construct a dialogue in which each pair of sentences is based on a pair of items/locations listed. The first sentence should be an informal (**du**) command to buy the item(s) somewhere; the second a response preferring (**lieber**) to buy them elsewhere. The first pair is provided.

1 anderthalb Pfund kleine
   feste Tomaten   auf dem Markt

   Hol bitte anderthalb Pfund kleine feste Tomaten
     vom Gemüsegeschäft.

   Die Tomaten kaufe ich lieber auf dem Markt.

2 ein kleines Weißbrot   im Supermarkt

3 250 Gramm gekochter Schinken in der Altstadt

4 ein Kopfsalat   auf dem Markt

5 zwanzig Eier   auf dem Markt

6 eine schöne Gurke   auf dem Markt

7 zehn frische Brötchen   im Supermarkt

8 ein halbes Pfund Hackfleisch   in der Altstadt

9 zehn Pfund Kartoffeln   auf dem Markt

10 ein Pfund grüne Bohnen   auf dem Markt

Week 8

- more on word order
- auxiliary verbs ("can," "must," "will," etc.) and how they are used with a main verb
- quantities and measurements
- verbs for "to be" and "to put" indicating position
- the use of **da(r)-** with prepositions to express "on it," "about them," etc.

8.1 MORE ON WORD ORDER

There are two contexts when a verb is in the first position in a German sentence: a command (**Kommen Sie sofort!** Come at once!) and a question.

Gehst du jetzt bitte einkaufen?
("Go you now please to shop?")

This question illustrates another rule about word order. It contains two verbs: **gehst** and **einkaufen**. In this case, the conjugated verb (here, **gehst**) is in the first position (in a question) or the second position (in a statement).

The verb it is used with to complete its meaning (here, **einkaufen**) is used in its infinitive (**-en**) form (e.g., "to shop"). Unlike in English, the two verbs are not found together. In German, the infinitive always comes at the end of the sentence (or question).

Remember that the introductory element might not be the subject. It could be a single word or a group of words, such as a direct object, an adverbial phrase, an expression of time or place, etc. Below are some other examples of the structure when two verbs are used to express something (**gehen**, conjugated + infinitive):

Ich gehe zweimal in der Woche schwimmen.
("I go twice in the week to swim.")
Gehen wir morgen Abend mit der Gruppe essen?
("Go we tomorrow evening with the group to eat?")

Meine Mutter geht immer früh schlafen.
("My mother goes always early to sleep.")
Manchmal gehen wir stundenlang im Wald spazieren.*
("Sometimes go we for hours in the forest to walk.")
(*Other elements in the sentence that give information about TIME–MANNER–PLACE must appear in that order.)

8.2 AUXILIARY VERBS: "CAN," "MUST," "WILL," ETC.

Let's look at some auxiliary verbs, to which the rules described in section 8.1 apply. Auxiliary verbs are used to modify the way a main verb is understood. They include modal verbs (which express necessity, possibility, ability, etc.: e.g., "can," "must," "may") as well as verbs used to indicate information about the tense (e.g., "will").

Eight key auxiliary verbs (**dürfen** may, **können** can, **müssen** must, **sollen** should, **mögen** like to, **wollen** want to, **lassen** let, and **werden** will) are listed below with their conjugations in the present tense. They are all irregular and are frequently used with other verbs, so it is very useful to learn them.

8

	dürfen to be allowed to (permission)	**können** to be able to (possibility)
ich/er/sie(she)/**es**	**darf**	**kann**
du (inf. sing.)	**darfst**	**kannst**
wir/Sie/sie(they)	**dürfen**	**können**
ihr (inf. pl.)	**dürft**	**könnt**

	mögen to like to (also "may")	**müssen** to have to (obligation)
ich/er/sie(she)/**es**	**mag**	**muss**
du (inf. sing.)	**magst**	**musst**
wir/Sie/sie(they)	**mögen**	**müssen**
ihr (inf. pl.)	**mögt**	**müsst**

	sollen to be supposed to (should)	wollen to want to, to intend to
ich/er/sie(she)**/es**	**soll**	**will**
du (inf. sing.)	**sollst**	**willst**
wir/Sie/sie(they)	**sollen**	**wollen**
ihr (inf. pl.)	**sollt**	**wollt**
	lassen to let/allow to	werden will (future)
ich	**lasse**	**werde**
du (inf. sing.)	**lässt**	**wirst**
er/sie(she)**/es**	**lässt**	**wird**
wir/Sie/sie(they)	**lassen**	**werden**
ihr (inf. pl.)	**lasst**	**werdet**

8.3 USING AUXILIARY VERBS

(1) dürfen: to be allowed to (permission), may/mustn't

Darf ich hier rauchen?
Can I smoke here?
Darf ich meinen Freund vorstellen?
May I introduce my friend?
In der Kirche darf man nicht laut reden.
One mustn't talk loudly in church.

(2) können: to be able to (possibility), can

**Für seine sechs Jahre kann er sehr gut
schwimmen.**
He can swim very well considering he's only six.
Seine Rede kann noch lange dauern.
His speech may go on for a long time yet.
Wir können seine Experimente nicht finanzieren.
We aren't able to finance his experiments.

(3) mögen: to like, also may (possibility)

Er mag wohl reich sein, er kommt trotzdem nicht in den Club.
He may well be rich, but he's still not going to get into the club.
Ich mag nicht über alles klagen, aber ...
I don't like complaining about everything, but ...

(4) müssen: to have to (obligation), must/needn't

Ich muss um zwölf zu Hause sein, sonst kommt das Mittagessen zu spät auf den Tisch.
I must be home at twelve, or else I'll be late getting lunch on the table.
Dieser Brief ist an dich. Du musst nicht unbedingt antworten.
This letter is (addressed) to you. You aren't absolutely obliged to reply.

(5) sollen: to be supposed/expected to, should

Du sollst erst essen und dann ins Kino gehen.
You should eat first and then go to the movie.
Ich kann nicht länger auf ihn warten, er soll sofort kommen.
I can't wait for him any longer, he's to come at once.
Ich kann ihn empfehlen, er soll ein sehr guter Klavierlehrer sein.
I can recommend him. He's said to be a very good piano teacher.

(6) wollen: to want to, to intend to

Er ist vollkommen satt, er will nichts mehr essen.
He is completely full. He doesn't want to eat another thing.

8

Sie will gar nichts mehr von der Sache hören.
She doesn't want to hear anything more at all about
the matter.
Er will seine Ferien in den Bergen verbringen.
He intends to spend his vacation in the mountains.

(7) lassen: to let/allow someone to do, to get someone
to, to make/have someone do, to have something done

**Die Chefin lässt ihre Sekretärin unwichtige
Briefe unterschreiben.**
The boss gets her personal assistant to sign
unimportant letters.
Er lässt seinen Wagen alle zwei Tage waschen.
He has his car washed every other day.
Mein Vater lässt grüßen.
My father sends his regards.
**Wir lassen unsere Tochter nicht alleine zur
Schule gehen.**
We don't let our daughter walk to school on her own.

(8) werden: will (future tense auxiliary)

**Ich mache es jetzt, ich werde in den nächsten
Tagen keine Zeit haben.**
I'll do it now. I won't have any time in the next few days.
Es ist schrecklich dunkel, es wird bestimmt regnen.
It's terribly dark. It's definitely going to rain.

VOCABULARY 1

Read through these new words that are used in the conversation that follows:

	etwas	somewhat
das	**Übergewicht**	extra weight
	abnehmen	to slim, to lose weight
der	**Urlaub (-e)**	vacation(s)
	anziehen	to wear, to put on
	unbedingt	absolutely
	Recht haben	to be right
	schwer	heavy
	hoffentlich	hopefully
	richtig	right, correct
	vorsichtig	careful, cautious
der	**Arzt (¨e) /**	doctor
die	**Ärztin (-nen)**	
	mager	lean
der	**Reis**	rice
	passen	to fit
	vorig	last, previous
das	**Jahr (-e)**	year
	vernünftig	sensible
	weiß	I know, he/she knows (from **wissen**, to know)
	schneiden	to cut
	lecker	delicious
die	**Sahnesoße**	cream sauce
	allein	on their own
	schmecken	to taste (good)
	achten (auf)	to pay attention (to), to keep an eye (on)
der	**Semmelknödel (-)**	bread dumpling
das	**Essen (-)**	meal
das	**Bierchen (-)**	(nice) little beer
	Moment mal!	Hold on!
	zunehmen	to put on weight

8

At Monday breakfast: discussing the menu for the day's main meal

MUTTER Was sollen wir denn heute essen?

TOCHTER Nach dem Wochenende habe ich bestimmt etwas Übergewicht. Von heute an muss ich abnehmen. In vier Wochen fahren wir in den Urlaub, da will ich meine Bikinis anziehen können. [Zu ihrem Bruder] Rudi, du musst auch unbedingt abnehmen.

SOHN Du hast Recht, ich bin zu schwer. Ich darf in den nächsten Wochen keine Kartoffeln mehr essen. Und hoffentlich lassen wir kein Bier mehr ins Haus bringen!

VATER Ganz richtig. Mit fünfzig muss ich auch vorsichtiger sein. Der Arzt sagt, ich soll nur Fisch oder mageres Fleisch essen, dazu nur frisches Gemüse, keine Kartoffeln, keinen Reis.

MUTTER Was soll es denn geben? Ich passe nicht mehr in meine Sommerkleidung vom vorigen Jahr. Wir müssen vernünftig sein. Ich weiß was, ich lasse beim Metzger vier extra magere Steaks schneiden.

TOCHTER Ja, und dann brauchen wir dazu nur eine leckere Sahnesoße.

SOHN Fleisch und Sahnesoße allein schmecken nicht.

VATER Das mag sein, aber wir müssen auf die Kalorien achten.

SOHN Vielleicht können wir dann ein paar Semmelknödel und Karotten in Buttersoße dazu essen.

VATER Zu so einem Essen muss man ein kaltes Bierchen trinken, nicht?

MUTTER Moment mal, werden wir nicht auch von diesem Essen zunehmen?

MOTHER Well, what should we eat today?

DAUGHTER I definitely put on some extra weight after the weekend. I must lose weight from today onward. We're going on vacation in four weeks, and I want to be able to wear my bikinis. [To her brother] Rudi, you absolutely have to lose weight too.

SON You're right, I'm too heavy. I mustn't eat any potatoes in the next few weeks. And hopefully we won't be having any more beer brought into the house!

FATHER Quite right. At fifty I have to be more careful too. The doctor says I should only eat fish or lean meat, and with it only fresh vegetables; no potatoes and no rice.

MOTHER Well, what is it to be? I don't fit into my summer clothes from last year anymore. We have to be sensible. I know—I'll get four particularly lean steaks cut at the butcher's.

DAUGHTER Yes, and then we only need a delicious cream sauce with them.

SON Meat and cream sauce don't taste good on their own.

FATHER That may be, but we've got to keep an eye on the calories.

SON Then perhaps we can have a few dumplings and some carrots in butter sauce with them.

FATHER You have to drink a nice cold beer with a meal like that, don't you?

MOTHER Hold on, aren't we going to put on weight from this meal too?

8

Exercise 1

Insert the correct form of **dürfen, können,** or **müssen** in the following sentences, choosing the auxiliary verb that best fits the sense:

1 Sie ... gut Englisch sprechen, ihre Lehrerin ist gut.
2 Wir ... die Milch trinken, sonst wird sie schlecht.
3 Er ist sechzehn Jahre alt, er ... nicht Auto fahren.
4 Ich ... ins Geschäft gehen und einkaufen, wir haben heute Abend Freunde zu Besuch.
5 Er ... kein Bier trinken, er will abnehmen.
6 Die kleine Tochter ... den Film sehen, es ist Sonntag.
7 Das Mittagessen ... warten, sie will erst das Auto waschen.

8.4 MEASUREMENTS AND QUANTITIES

In English, "of" is required in expressions such as:

two meters of string   (measurements)
a big pile of trash   (quantities)
some cans of beans   (other units)

However, the corresponding expressions in German don't include any linking word:

zwei Meter Bindfaden
ein großer Haufen Abfall
einige Dosen Bohnen

If the first noun is m. or n., it is always in the singular, even when the meaning is plural:

Ich brauche für dieses Rezept zwei Tassen Mehl.
I need two cups of flour for this recipe.
Ich trinke jeden Tag drei Glas Wasser.
I drink three glasses of water every day.

8.5 THE EXPRESSIONS **ES IST** AND **ES SIND** ("THERE IS"/"THERE ARE")

In section 6.2, we saw the expression **es gibt**, which translates to "there is/are" to talk about something generally. When you know that something exists or is available and the dominant idea is its quantity or number or location, use **es ist/sind**:

Es ist ein Brief für dich da.
There's a letter for you here.
Es sind zwei Zeitungen für meine Mutter da.
There are two newspapers here for my mother.

Remember that **es gibt** is invariable and is used with a singular or plural noun, which is a DO. With **es ist/sind**, the verb has to agree with the real subject of the sentence (here, **Brief**, singular and **Zeitungen**, plural). So, the **es** is not the subject: the noun it refers to is. This noun thus needs to be in the nominative (SU) case.

8.6 VERBS FOR "TO BE" INDICATING POSITION

German has several verbs that describe the position of things, where in English, we typically just use "to be" (**sein**).

When talking about certain types of objects, choosing the appropriate verb isn't usually too tricky. Here are some examples with three of these verbs:

(1) When something is upright: **stehen** to stand

Auf dem Tisch steht eine alte Vase.
or   **Eine alte Vase steht auf dem Tisch.**
or   **Es steht eine alte Vase auf dem Tisch.**
There's an old vase on the table.
Der Fernseher steht in der Ecke.
The television is in the corner.

Note that sentences of this kind beginning with **es** (e.g., in the third example above) are only possible when the subject is a noun preceded by **(k)ein**, another indefinite word (e.g., **einige**), or nothing.

(2) When something is flat: **liegen** to lie

Auf dem Boden liegt ein schmutziger Teppich.
or   **Ein schmutziger Teppich liegt auf dem Boden.**
or   **Es liegt ein schmutziger Teppich auf dem Boden.**
There's a dirty carpet on the floor.
Die Zeitung liegt auf dem Wohnzimmertisch.
The newspaper is on the living room table.

(3) When something is inserted into, put inside, or concealed behind: **stecken** to stick into

Im Schloss steckt ein rostiger Schlüssel.
or   **Ein rostiger Schlüssel steckt im Schloss.**
or   **Es steckt ein rostiger Schlüssel im Schloss.**
There's a rusty key in the lock.

Was steckt hinter dem Vorhang?
What's behind the curtain?

8

8.7 VERBS FOR "TO PUT" INDICATING POSITION

Just as position can be specified with **stehen**, **liegen**, or **stecken**, the action of moving something to a position can be expressed either generally with **tun** (to put) or more specifically with **stellen**, **legen**, or **stecken**:

	to be in a position	to put in a position
general	**sein**	**tun**
upright	**stehen**	**stellen**
flat	**liegen**	**legen**
inserted	**stecken**	**stecken**

(1) General movement to a position: **tun** (to put, to do)

ich	**tue**
du (inf. sing.)	**tust**
er/sie(she)/**es**	**tut**
wir/Sie/sie(they)	**tun**
ihr (inf. pl.)	**tut**

Er tut seine Bücher immer auf das falsche Regal.
He always puts his books on the wrong shelf.
Sie tut etwas Milch in die Milchkanne.
She's putting a little milk in the milk jug.

(2) To stand something upright: **stellen**

Wir stellen den Nachttisch neben das Bett.
We'll put the bedside table next to the bed.
Er stellt die leeren Flaschen vor die Tür.
He puts the empty bottles outside the door.

8

(3) To lay something down: **legen**

Sie legt einen Fünfzigeuroschein auf die Theke.
She put a fifty euro note on the counter.

(4) To insert something into, to stick inside, or to conceal: **stecken**

Er steckt gerade einen Zehneuroschein in deine Manteltasche!
He's just putting a ten euro note in your coat pocket!

8.8 MORE ABOUT PREPOSITIONS

With all of the prepositions we saw in section 6.1 (1)–(3), except **ohne** and **seit**, normally a following pronoun would only refer to a person. To refer to something other than a living being after a preposition, the pronoun is replaced with **da(r)-** + preposition.

This construction forms one word (e.g., **darüber**, **damit**), with the stress on the preposition. The **-r-** is used when the preposition begins with a vowel.

Compare:
Ich lache über sie.
I'm laughing at them. (e.g., my children, **meine Kinder**)
Ich lache darüber.
I'm laughing at them. (e.g., my mistakes, **meine Fehler**)

These **da(r)-** + preposition terms don't decline: they are invariable.

They can stand for a singular or a plural noun, which could be a thing or a fact or an idea.

A: Ich höre, er ist arbeitslos.
B: Ja, aber er redet nie darüber.
A: I hear he's unemployed.
B: Yes, but he never talks about it.
(i.e., about being unemployed)

Some combinations of **da(r)-** + preposition have acquired permanent meanings of their own:

dafür	instead, on the other hand
dagegen	by contrast, on the other hand
daher	therefore
damit	so that, in order that
darum	therefore

As for the exceptions, **ohne** (without) is simply followed by the standard pronouns (see section 3.2).

To say "since that," "since it," or "since then" using **seit**, the term is **seitdem**.

8

Exercise 2

Insert the most appropriate word from the column on the right into the gap in each of the following sentences. You may need to juggle with the **da(r)-** words so you only use each one once.

1 Er hat eine Feile in der Hand, … öffnet er die Tür. — dazwischen

2 Vor dem Einbrecher ist eine Treppe, … sitzt ein Skelett. — danach

3 Wir trinken ein Glas Wasser, … gehen wir schlafen. — darauf

4 Ich esse eine Wurst, … trinke ich eine Cola. — daneben

5 Ich nehme fünf Rosen, … muss ich €10,75 bezahlen. — dahinter

6 Auf der Tischdecke liegt ein Brot, … steht ein Glas. — dazu

7 Der junge Mann ist arbeitslos, … muss er etwas tun. — damit

8 Sie sehen die Kirche und das Gasthaus, Sie nehmen die Straße … — dagegen

9 Das Haus steht direkt an der Straße, der Garten liegt … — davor

10 Wir wollen einkaufen gehen, … müssen wir noch essen. — dafür

VOCABULARY 2

	Pass auf!	Now look!
der	Kühlschrank (¨e)	refrigerator
	möglichst	as far/much as possible
	freihalten	to keep clear
das	Hähnchen (-)	chicken
die	Himbeertorte (-n)	raspberry flan
das	Fertigessen (-)	oven-ready meal
das	Eisfach (¨er)	freezer
	morgen	tomorrow
	übermorgen	the day after tomorrow
der	Pflaumenkuchen (-)	plum tart
die	Schüssel (-n)	dish
die	Schlagsahne	whipped cream (also whipping cream)
der	Becher (-)	carton (also beaker, mug)
die	Packung (-en)	pack, packet
die	Leberwurst (¨e)	liver sausage
	einzeln	singly, separately
das	Stück	piece (but with number sometimes omitted in translation)
	zum Weichwerden	to get soft
	flach	flat
der	Behälter (-)	container
der	Scheibenkäse	cheese in slices
der	Salat	lettuce, salad
die	Weintraube (-n)	grape
der	Beutel (-)	bag
die	Apfelsine (-n)	orange
der	Blumenkohl	cauliflower
der	Rosenkohl	Brussels sprouts
das	Gemüsefach (¨er)	vegetable drawer
das	Glas (¨er)	jar
der	Honig	honey
die	Erdbeermarmelade	strawberry jam
	Meine Güte!	My goodness!
das	Obst	fruit

8

Exercise 3

Complete the monologue by filling the spaces with the appropriate words for "be" and "put." Do this exercise twice, first using the general **sein** and **tun**, and then using the more precise verbs from sections 8.6 and 8.7. The vocabulary you need is on page 105.

A daughter with elderly parents is about to leave town on business for a few days and tells her father what she has left in the refrigerator for them.

Pass auf! Ich werde den Kühlschrank möglichst frei-halten. Dann kannst du alles ganz leicht finden. Das Hähnchen für Sonntag, die gefrorene Himbeertorte und die beiden Fertigessen (1) … / … ich ins Eisfach. Die Fertigessen kannst du morgen und übermorgen essen. Der Pflaumenkuchen und die Schüssel mit Schlagsahne (2) … / … oben. Da (3) … / … ich auch die beiden Flaschen Wein hin … Ach, da ist gerade noch etwas Platz, den Becher Joghurt kann ich dazwischen (4) … / … Die vier Flaschen Bier (5) … / … ich unten in die Tür, und zwei Packungen Milch (6) … / … daneben. Ich (7) … / … die Packung gekochten Schinken, die Salami und die Leberwurst in die Mitte. Sie sind natürlich für abends … Eier? … Die Eier (8) … / … ich natürlich einzeln oben in die Tür, zwölf Stück. Zwei Stück Butter (9) … / … ich in das obere Fach in der Tür, das Dritte lasse ich draußen zum Weichwerden. Der flache Behälter mit drei Sorten Käse (10) … / … in der Mitte, und dahinter liegen eine Tube Mayonnaise und der Scheibenkäse. Die Gurke, der Salat, die Weintrauben und die Tomaten (11) … / … unten, und den Beutel Apfelsinen, einen Kopf Blumenkohl und den Rosenkohl (12) … / … ich ins Gemüsefach ganz unten. Ein kleines Glas Honig und ein Glas Erdbeermarmelade (13) … / … ich weiter oben in die Tür … Meine Güte, ist der Kühlschrank wieder voll!

Exercise 4

Now, translate the monologue from Exercise 3.

Week 9

- *further meanings and uses of* **der, die, das**
- *more about the use of the present tense*
- *irregular present-tense forms of some common verbs*
- *the present-perfect tense to talk about the past*
- *time expressions, including months, days, dates, and times of day*

9.1 MORE ABOUT DER, DIE, DAS

(1) das not only is the definite article "the" for neuter nouns but can also be used as the pronoun "that":

(i) **A: Du sollst heute bezahlen.**
   You're supposed to pay today.
   B: Das weiß ich. I know (that).

(ii) **A: Zehn Brötchen kosten vier Euro.**
   Ten rolls cost four euros.
   B: Das ist zu teuer. That's too much.

In the above, **das** is a direct object in (i) and the subject in (ii). It refers to an idea rather than an identifiable noun.

(2) der (m.), **die** (f.), and **die** (plural) can also be used as pronouns to mean **er** (m.), **sie** (f.), and **sie** (plural):

(i) **A: Der Kellner hat unsere Bestellung seit einer Stunde.**
   The waiter has had our order for an hour.
   B: Der ist aber langsam! He's so slow!

(ii) **A: Ich warte auf die Schwester.**
   I'm waiting for the nurse.
   B: Die kommt heute nicht. She's not coming today.

(iii) **A: Was kosten Bananen?**
   What's the price of bananas?
   B: Die sind diese Woche billig.
   They're cheap this week.

This use of **der** and **die** so dominates the speech of some Germans that it almost replaces **er** and **sie**. When employed in this way, these pronouns tend to be used to start sentences and so are less common in questions, where this is not possible. They always have some degree of emphasis when spoken with this meaning, unlike when they are used to mean "the."

(3) The nominative (SU) uses described in (1) and (2) also apply in the accusative (DO) and dative (IO) cases:

	singular			plural
	m.	f.	n.	
DO	**den (ihn)**	**die (sie)**	**das**	**die (sie)**
IO	**dem (ihm)**	**der (ihr)**	**dem**	**denen (ihnen)**

Examples:

A: **Geben Sie mir den Schlüssel.**
Give me the key.

B: **Den finde ich im Augenblick nicht.** (m. DO)
I can't find it at the moment.

A: **Der Chef verspricht mir immer wieder mehr Geld.**
The boss is always promising me more money.

B: **Dem kann man gar nichts mehr glauben.** (m. IO)
You can't believe anything at all that he says.

A: **Diese Milch ist sauer.**
This milk is sour.

B: **Die müssen wir wegwerfen.** (f. DO)
We'll have to throw it away.

A: **Frau Klimpel schwatzt sehr viel.**
Mrs. Klimpel gossips a lot.

B: **Ja, der erzähle ich nie (et)was.** (f. IO)
Yes, I never tell her anything.

A: **Er verkauft sein Geschäft.**
He's selling his shop.

B: **Wie bitte? Das glaube ich nicht.** (n. DO)
What! I don't believe it.

A: **Er hat zu viele Probleme mit seinem Geschäft.**
He has too many problems with his business.

9

B: Dem ist er einfach nicht mehr gewachsen. (n. IO)
He simply can't cope (i.e., with the general situation)
any more.

A: Drüben sitzen die neuen Nachbarn.
The new neighbors are sitting over there.

B: Die kennen wir leider noch nicht. (plural DO)
Unfortunately we don't know them yet.

**A: Ich höre, die Kinder kriegen ein neues
Geschwisterchen.**
I hear the children are going to get a new
little brother or sister.

**B: Denen wollen wir aber eine Zeitlang noch
nichts davon sagen.** (plural IO)
We won't tell them anything (about it) for a
while, though.

(4) der and **die** are often used, particularly in spoken
German, before a first name or a family name to refer
to individuals. With first names, this may imply intimacy,
and with family names, it may have pejorative overtones:

Der Rudi muss jetzt nach Hause gehen.
Rudi has to go home now.
Ich sehe die Anna heute Abend.
I'm seeing Anna this evening.
Dem Thomas schenke ich fünf Euro.
I'll give Thomas five euros.
Der Schmidt lässt seine Kunden immer warten.
Schmidt is always keeping his customers waiting.

This usage has no parallel in English. The English "the"
before a family name, to mean a couple or family with
that name, is entirely optional in German:

(Die) Schmidts sind nicht zu Hause.
The Schmidts are not at home.

(5) A single **der**, **die**, or **das** can never suffice to cover a
series of nouns, particularly if they are of mixed gender

or number. But in both conversation and writing, it is common practice to omit **der**, **die**, **das** altogether with groups of two or more nouns, even if separated by **und**:

Das Frühstück ist fertig. Brot, Butter, Eier, Marmelade, Honig, Kaffee, Milch, Zucker, Salz und Pfeffer stehen auf dem Tisch.
Breakfast is ready. The bread, butter, eggs, jam, honey, coffee, milk, sugar, salt, and pepper are on the table.

Exercise 1

Insert the correct declension of **der**, **die**, or **das** in the following sentences.

1 A Wie geht es den Geschwistern?
   B Von … hören wir gar nichts.

2 A Wie lange müssen wir auf den Kaffee warten?
   B … ist schon lange fertig!

3 Der Junge bekommt immer soviel Geld von mir. … gebe ich jetzt nichts mehr.

4 A Bei diesem Wetter kann man gar nicht gut arbeiten.
   B … sage ich auch.

5 A Unsere Tochter heiratet nächste Woche.
   B … wünsche ich viel Spaß!

6 A Wie alt ist der Sohn von der Wirtin?
   B … weiß ich nicht.

7 A Wie alt ist der Sohn von der Wirtin?
   B … kenne ich nicht.

8 A Ich lese gern die Sonntagszeitung.
   B … lese ich auch gern.

9 A Meine Eltern sind krank, aber sie wollen nicht zum Arzt.
   B … kann man aber auch gar nicht helfen!

10 A Herr Schmidt verkauft mir saure Milch.
   B Bei … kaufe ich nichts mehr!

9.2 USES OF THE PRESENT TENSE

(1) The present tense in German is used for any situations taking place in the present as well as ongoing actions, including actions you're in the middle of (the present continuous, as in the second sentence below):

I go to my mother's twice a week.
I'm going home.

It's also used to express an action that will occur in the future, if this seems like a clear extension of the present:

Nächsten Monat fahre ich in die Vereinigten Staaten.
I'm going to the United States next month.
Ich fahre mit meinem Bruder in Urlaub.
I'm going on vacation with my brother.

(2) When the future is more open, relying more on intention or conviction, the future tense with **werden** (conjugated in the present) and the infinitive is used:

Ich werde nicht mehr so viel trinken.
I'm going to drink less.
Bei solcher Inflation wird alles bald viel mehr kosten.
With inflation like this, everything's going to cost a lot more soon.

Sometimes the future with **werden** is necessary for clarity. For example, the following request

Können Sie mir helfen, ich suche meine Koffer.
Can you help me? I'm looking for my suitcases.

could have an answer in the present tense:

Ich helfe Ihnen.
I'll help you.

9

Here, the present tense has a clear future meaning, the implication being **sofort** or **gleich** (at once), which might be added. But if the intended meaning is "I'll do my best," the present tense could be misleading ("I'm doing my best"), and the future with **werden** is preferable:

Ich werde mein Bestes tun. I'll do my best.

(3) Used with a time reference, the present tense indicates a state of affairs continuing from the past into the present (English requires the present perfect in this context).

Ich kenne ihn seit sechs Jahren.
I have known him for six years.
Wie lange wohnen Sie schon hier?
How long have you been living here?
Wir wohnen hier seit 2012.
We've been living here since 2012.

9.3 PRESENT TENSE: IRREGULAR VERBS

There are several common verbs that are irregular in the present tense in the second- and third-person singular. Some of these key verbs are listed below, grouped according to the sound change in the stem vowel that occurs. Only the third-person singular is given. The second person (**du**) is formed by inserting **-s-** before the final **-t** (unless the stem ends in **-s**, **-ss**, or **-ß**):

infinitive		3rd-person singular
fahren	to go (by means of transportation), to travel	**fährt** he/she/it goes
fallen	to fall	**fällt**
halten	to hold	**hält**
schlafen	to sleep	**schläft**
schlagen	to beat, to hit	**schlägt**
tragen	to carry, to wear	**trägt**
verlassen	to leave	**verlässt**
wachsen	to grow	**wächst**

laufen	to run	**läuft**
lesen	to read	**liest**
sehen	to see	**sieht**
stehlen	to steal	**stiehlt**
essen	to eat	**isst**
geben	to give	**gibt**
helfen	to help	**hilft**
nehmen	to take	**nimmt**
sprechen	to speak	**spricht**
vergessen	to forget	**vergisst**
werfen	to throw	**wirft**

One common verb is irregular throughout the singular:

wissen	to know (a fact)	**ich/er/sie/es weiß**
		du weißt

9.4 THE PRESENT PERFECT

This tense is formed in English with the auxiliary verb "to have" + past participle of the main verb (e.g., "I have lived"). We'll look at the uses of the present perfect in section 9.6. First, let's look at how it's formed in German.

The good news is that it is also formed with the auxiliary verb **haben** plus a past participle (however, with certain verbs, **sein** is the auxiliary: more on this in section 9.5).

As we've seen, when two verbs are used together, the conjugated verb is the second element of the sentence (or the first or second in a question), and the main verb—in this case, the past participle—moves to the end of the sentence (see sections 8.2–8.3 for a reminder).

In English, a regular past participle is formed by adding -ed to the verb (e.g., helped, climbed), although there are many irregular past participles (e.g., made, done, become, been, thrown, etc.).

9

For most verbs, the past participle is formed in German by putting the prefix **ge-** before the stem and replacing the **-en** of the infinitive ending with **-t**. For example:
machen (to make)→ **ge-mach-t**→ **gemacht** (made)

If the stem of the verb ends in **t** or **d**, an **-e-** is inserted before the added **-t** for pronunciation reasons:
warten (to wait)→ **ge-wart-et**→ **gewartet** (waited)

Note the word order of the two verbs:

Wir haben ein Bild gemalt.

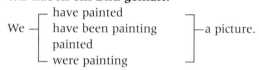

Wir sind in die Küche gerast.

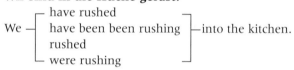

9.5 WHICH AUXILIARY: **SEIN** OR **HABEN**?

Usually, **haben** is the auxiliary in the perfect tenses. However, in the two contexts below, **sein** is the auxiliary:

(1) If the main verb (i.e., the verb used as the past participle) denotes a process involving motion or a change of state: e.g., **kommen** (to come); **springen** (to jump); **sterben** (to die); **werden** (to become). However, this does not include verbs with an explicit or implied direct object, such as **bringen** (to take, to bring); **reichen** (to hand); **schicken** (to send); **ziehen** (to pull).

(2) If the main verb is either **sein** (to be) or **bleiben** (to stay, to remain): somewhat counterintuitively, these take **sein** as the auxiliary even though they imply the opposite of motion or a change of state.

Examples:

Ich bin hin und her gelaufen. (motion)
I ran (or walked) to and fro.
Ich bin zur Schule gegangen (motion)**, aber mein Bruder ist zu Hause geblieben** (from **bleiben**).
I went to school, but my brother stayed at home.
Meine Großmutter ist vier Wochen krank gewesen (from **sein**).
My grandmother was ill for four weeks.
Dann ist sie gestorben. (change of state)
Then she died.

As a result, certain verbs can take either **sein** or **haben**, according to the meaning. For example, **fahren**:

Wir sind immer mit dem Zug gefahren. (no DO)
We always went by train.
Er hat einen eleganten Sportwagen gefahren. (DO)
He was driving an elegant sports car.

Note that all the past participles above are irregular—these generally end in **-en**.

9.6 USES OF THE PRESENT PERFECT

9

In German, the present perfect is used to talk about any event that happened in the past. It is more flexible than the equivalent in English, which is only used if something happened at an indefinite time or started in the past and is continuing into the present. Thus, the German present perfect can have a wide variety of meanings:

We have bought a house.
We have been buying a house.
We bought a house.
We were buying a house.

To convey any of these meanings, the German is simply:

Wir haben ein Haus gekauft.

As we've seen, most verbs form the past participle by adding **ge_(e)t** to the stem. This is the case for most words originating from non-German sources (e.g., **gestartet, gestoppt, gelandet, gecheckt**).

Here are some examples of the standard pattern:

infinitive		stem	past participle
kaufen	to buy	**kauf**	**gekauft** (bought)
machen	to make, do	**mach**	**gemacht** (made, done)
sagen	to say	**sag**	**gesagt** (said)
zählen	to count	**zähl**	**gezählt** (counted)
baden	to bathe	**bad**	**gebadet** (bathed)
blenden	to dazzle	**blend**	**geblendet** (dazzled)
bluten	to bleed	**blut**	**geblutet** (bled)
leisten	to achieve	**leist**	**geleistet** (achieved)

But we also mentioned that some verbs don't follow this pattern.

(1) Irregular past participles

Helpfully, an irregular past participle in German often corresponds to an irregular form of an English verb from the same source (e.g., **schwimmen** to swim, **geschwommen** swum).

Here are the main irregular past participles, grouped according to the changes that occur. Any particular oddities are underlined.

infinitive		past participle
brennen	to burn	**gebrannt**
bringen	to bring, to take	**gebra<u>ch</u>t**
denken	to think	**geda<u>ch</u>t**
kennen	to know (someone)	**gekannt**
wissen	to know (a fact)	**gewusst**
essen	to eat	**gegessen**
fahren	to go (by transport)	**gefahren**
fangen	to catch	**gefangen**

geben	to give	**gegeben**
halten	to hold	**gehalten**
kommen	to come	**gekommen**
laufen	to run	**gelaufen**
lesen	to read	**gelesen**
messen	to measure	**gemessen**
rufen	to call (out)	**gerufen**
schlafen	to sleep	**geschlafen**
schlagen	to hit, to beat	**geschlagen**
sehen	to see	**gesehen**
stoßen	to bump	**gestoßen**
tragen	to carry, to wear	**getragen**
treten	to step	**getreten**
wachsen	to grow	**gewachsen**
stehen	to stand	**gestanden**
gehen	to go	**gegangen**
brechen	to break	**gebrochen**
helfen	to help	**geholfen**
sprechen	to speak	**gesprochen**
sterben	to die	**gestorben**
treffen	to meet	**getroffen**
werden	to become	**geworden**
nehmen	to take	**genommen**
stehlen	to steal	**gestohlen**
leiden	to suffer	**gelitten**
pfeifen	to whistle	**gepfiffen**
schneiden	to cut	**geschnitten**
streiten	to quarrel	**gestritten**
bleiben	to stay, remain	**geblieben**
leihen	to lend	**geliehen**
scheinen	to seem, shine	**geschienen**
schreiben	to write	**geschrieben**
steigen	to climb	**gestiegen**
treiben	to drive, impel	**getrieben**

9

sitzen	to sit	**gese<u>ss</u>en**
schwimmen	to swim	**geschwommen**
finden	to find	**gefunden**
sinken	to sink	**gesunken**
springen	to jump	**gesprungen**
trinken	to drink	**getrunken**
bitten	to ask, request	**gebeten**
riechen	to smell	**gerochen**
schließen	to shut, close	**geschlossen**
liegen	to lie (recline)	**gelegen**
bieten	to offer	**geboten**
fliegen	to fly	**geflogen**
fliehen	to flee	**geflohen**
ziehen	to pull, draw	**gezogen**
lügen	to lie (fib)	**gelogen**
sein	to be	**ge<u>wes</u>en**

(2) Effect of prefixes on the past participle

Many German words are composites, consisting of a central core with a distinctive meaning (the root), to which further syllables can be attached before or after. In the case of an infinitive, such as **bekommen** (to get), the structure looks like this:

be	+	**komm**	+	**en**
prefix	+	root	+	suffix

The prefix, attached to the front, combines with the root to produce the overall meaning of the verb. The root provides the core meaning of the verb. The suffix, attached to the end, is the ending that identifies the form of the verb.

Suffixes thus typically indicate the tense and the person of the conjugation. Verbs with a prefix form the past participle differently from the patterns we have seen.

Verbs with an inseparable prefix don't take the prefix **ge-**. (As their name implies, these are verbs whose prefix always remains attached to the front of the verb.)

Some key inseparable-prefix verbs and their past participles are listed below. The stressed syllables are underlined, as this is important in the pronunciation. Note that the prefix is unstressed.

TYPE I: INSEPARABLE-PREFIX VERBS

infinitive	past participle	prefix	root	suffix
bekommen	**bekommen**	be	**komm**	en
to get	got/gotten			
empfinden	**empfunden**	emp	**fund**	en
to feel	felt			
entsprechen	**entsprochen**	ent	**sproch**	en
to correspond	corresponded			
erwarten	**erwartet**	er	**wart**	et
to expect	expected			
gehören	**gehört**	ge	**hör**	t
to belong	belonged			
misslingen	**misslungen**	miss	**lung**	en
to fail	failed			
verstehen	**verstanden**	ver	**stand**	en
to understand	understood			
widersprechen	**widersprochen**	wider	**sproch**	en
to contradict	contradicted			
zerstören	**zerstört**	zer	**stör**	t
to destroy	destroyed			

9

In contrast, verbs with separable prefixes form their past participle by inserting the **-ge-** after the prefix and before the root. (Separable-prefix verbs are those with a prefix that detaches from the stem and moves to the last position in the sentence in present-tense statements.)

Some separable-prefix verbs and their past participles are listed below. Note that the prefix is stressed.

TYPE II: SEPARABLE-PREFIX VERBS

infinitive	past participle	prefixes		root	suffix
ankommen to arrive	**angekommen** arrived	**an**	ge	komm	en
aufstehen to stand up	**aufgestanden** stood up	**auf**	ge	stand	en
ausmachen to switch off	**ausgemacht** switched off	**aus**	ge	mach	t
beitreten to join	**beigetreten** joined	**bei**	ge	tret	en
einladen to invite	**eingeladen** invited	**ein**	ge	lad	en
gegenzeichnen to countersign	**gegengezeichnet** countersigned	**gegen**	ge	zeichn	et
mithelfen to assist	**mitgeholfen** assisted	**mit**	ge	holf	en
nachholen to catch up	**nachgeholt** caught up	**nach**	ge	hol	t
vorbeugen to avert	**vorgebeugt** averted	**vor**	ge	beug	t
zuhören to listen	**zugehört** listened	**zu**	ge	hör	t

The past participle of both types of verbs is written as a single word, e.g., **verstanden** (understood), **ausgemacht** (switched off).

So, how do you know which suffix to add for the past participle in these contexts? In both types of verbs, follow this rule: if the corresponding verb without a prefix is irregular (e.g., **stehen** to stand → **gestanden** stood), any related verbs with prefixes take the same irregularity (e.g., **aufstehen** to stand up → **aufgestanden** stood up; **verstehen** to understand → **verstanden** understood).

The two preceding tables contain the main prefixes that are used exclusively as inseparable or separable prefixes, but they are not exhaustive.

There are some prefixes (e.g., **über**, **um**, **unter**) that can be inseparable or separable, producing verbs with completely different meanings: e.g., **umbauen** (to build around, to enclose); **umbauen** (to rebuild, to convert).

To help you identify and use these verbs correctly, all verbs with prefixes are labeled (I) or (II) in the mini-dictionary and in the vocabulary lists from now on.

(3) Verbs ending in **-ieren**

All verbs with an infinitive ending in **-ieren** (note the stress) (e.g., **telefonieren**, **kontrollieren**, **interessieren**, **informieren**) form the past participle without the **ge-**, but with the **-t** (e.g., **telefoniert**, etc.).

9

Exercise 2

For each sentence, insert the correct form of **sein** or **haben** in the first gap and the past participle of the given main verb in the second gap.

1 Er ... mir den Schlüssel ... (bringen)

2 Mein Freund ... heute in die Vereinigten Staaten ... (fliegen)

3 Unsere Eltern ... vor einigen Jahren ... (sterben)

4 Meine Mutter ... die Erdbeermarmelade in den Kühlschrank ... (stellen)

5 Das Kind ... vom Tisch ... (springen)

6 Ich ... heute den ganzen Tag zu Hause ... (bleiben)

7 Dieses Jahr ... die Miete für unsere Wohnung sehr ... (steigen)

8 Ich ... meiner Wirtin einen Brief ... (schicken)

9 Wir ... von meiner Schwester Geld ... (bekommen)

10 Du ... wirklich sehr groß ... (werden)

9

9.8 TIME EXPRESSIONS

(1) Expressions for frequency

nie	never
je (jemals)	ever
selten	rarely
einmal	once
zweimal	twice (**dreimal** three times, etc.)
ab und zu	occasionally
manchmal	sometimes
regelmäßig	regularly
immer wieder	again and again
immer	always

(2) General expressions for "now"

jetzt	now (can refer to what is happening or what is imminent)
nun	now (the final step in a series: also has the nontemporal sense of "well now")
im Augenblick **augenblicklich** **im Moment** **momentan**	at the moment
eben **gerade**	just now (a moment ago); right now (at the moment); now, just (presently, in a moment) (as with "just," **eben** and **gerade** often also mean "simply" or "barely")
vorhin	a short while ago
neulich	recently (but only in the sense of a particular recent occasion in the speaker's mind)
letztens **in letzter Zeit**	recently
vor einiger Zeit	some time ago
sofort, gleich	right away, immediately, at once
bald	soon
nachher	afterward

(3) General expressions related to "then"

dann	then
damals	at that time
davor, vorher	before that
kurz davor	shortly before that

danach	after that, afterward
kurz danach	shortly afterward
früher	formerly

(4) Time measured from now

vor einem Monat	a month ago
vor einer Woche	a week ago
seit fünf Sekunden	for five seconds (i.e., starting five seconds ago)
in drei Tagen	in three days (i.e., after three days)

(5) Time measured from then

einen Monat davor	a month before, previously
einen Monat zuvor	

seit vier Jahren	for four years (i.e., starting four years previously)

nach zwei Wochen	two weeks later
zwei Wochen danach	
zwei Wochen später	

(6) Expressions related to "today"

heute	today
gestern	yesterday
vorgestern	the day before yesterday

heute vor einer Woche	a week ago today
heute vor acht Tagen	

gestern vor zwei Wochen	two weeks ago yesterday
gestern vor vierzehn Tagen	

morgen	tomorrow
übermorgen	the day after tomorrow

heute in drei Wochen	three weeks from today
morgen in acht Tagen	a week from tomorrow

YEARS, MONTHS, DAYS, DATES, AND TIME

(1) Years (see also section 4.2): no preposition, or more formally, preceded by **im Jahre**:

2030 werde ich zwanzig. I'll be twenty in 2030.
or
Er hat im Jahre 2015 geheiratet. He got married in 2015.

seit/vor/nach 2020 since/before/after 2020

(2) Seasons: preposition **in** (all are m. nouns, so usually **im**)

	Frühling		spring
im	**Sommer**	in	summer
	Herbst		autumn
	Winter		winter

(3) Months: preposition **in** (all are m. nouns, so usually **im**)

	Januar		**Juli**
	Februar		**August**
im	**März**	**im**	**September**
	April		**Oktober**
	Mai		**November**
	Juni		**Dezember**

9

(4) Days: preposition **an** (all are m. nouns, so usually **am**)

	Sonntag		Sunday
	Montag		Monday
	Dienstag		Tuesday
am	**Mittwoch**	on	Wednesday
	Donnerstag		Thursday
	Freitag		Friday
	Sonnabend		Saturday
	or **Samstag**		

(5) Dates

Without the preposition "of," but with a full stop after the number to indicate it is an ordinal number:

Heute ist der 1. März. (erste) Today is March 1.
Donnerstag ist der 3. Mai. (dritte)
Morgen ist der 7. November. (siebte)
Freitag ist der 19. Juli. (neunzehnte)
Übermorgen ist der 20. Oktober. (zwanzigste)

Dating a letter or document:

den 2. Januar 2021 (zweiten) (accusative case: DO)
den 30.8.2021 (dreißigsten Achten) (as above)

With preposition **an**:

Am 15. Juni fahren wir in Urlaub. (fünfzehnten)
We're going on vacation on June 15.

(6) Time of day: preposition **um**

8.00	**acht Uhr**
8.05	**fünf nach acht**
8.08	**acht Minuten nach acht**
8.10	**zehn nach acht**
8.15	**Viertel nach acht** or **viertel neun**
8.20	**zwanzig nach acht**
8.25	**fünf vor halb neun**
8.30	**halb neun**
8.32	**zwei Minuten nach halb neun**
8.35	**fünf nach halb neun**
8.40	**zwanzig vor neun**
8.45	**Viertel vor neun** or **drei viertel neun**

Um Viertel nach eins kommt der Arzt.
The doctor's coming at a quarter past one.

The 24-hour clock, which is frequently used in timetables and other official contexts, is straightforward:

| 14.30 | vierzehn Uhr dreißig |
| 22.27 | zweiundzwanzig Uhr siebenundzwanzig |

Exercise 3

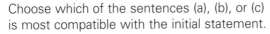

Choose which of the sentences (a), (b), or (c) is most compatible with the initial statement.

1 Im Augenblick habe ich keine Zeit.
   (a) Ich spiele in zwei Stunden Tennis.
   (b) Ich habe jetzt viel Arbeit.
   (c) Ich schlafe im Augenblick.

2 In zwei Wochen fahre ich in die Vereinigten Staaten.
   (a) Ich bin für zwei Wochen in den Vereinigten Staaten.
   (b) Der Urlaub in den Vereinigten Staaten ist zwei Wochen.
   (c) Ich fahre heute in vierzehn Tagen in die Vereinigten Staaten.

3 Übermorgen muss ich beim Metzger einkaufen.
   (a) In zwei Tagen kaufe ich ein Pfund Hackfleisch.
   (b) Übermorgen verkauft der Metzger sein Geschäft.
   (c) Übermorgen verkaufe ich Gemüse.

4 Seit gestern vor vierzehn Tagen ist seine Mutter krank.
   (a) Seine Mutter ist in vierzehn Tagen krank.
   (b) Seine Mutter ist schon zwei Wochen krank.
   (c) Vor vierzehn Tagen ist seine Mutter im Bett geblieben.

5 Vera ist eben in die Stadt gegangen.
   (a) Vera ist momentan in der Stadt.
   (b) Gerade ist Vera in die Stadt gefahren.
   (c) Vera will gleich in der Stadt spazieren gehen.

6 Früher hat Martin Bücher geschrieben.
   (a) Neulich hat Martin Bücher geschrieben.
   (b) Nachher schreibt Martin Bücher.
   (c) Martin hat damals gute Bücher geschrieben.

9

9.9 NICHT WAHR?, ETC.

In English, we frequently use question tags, which are basically a request for confirmation. These are determined by the verb that has been used:

He likes the painting, doesn't he?
So he likes the painting, does he?
He won't buy it, will he?
We won't pay, will we?
We're not going to pay, are we?

Or a question tag that suits all contexts would be "Right?" This is the approach taken in German, although the tag varies from region to region as well as according to the degree of formality.

The most formal tag, which can also be used in writing, is **..., nicht wahr?** ("not true?")

The most frequently used form is a shortened version of this: **..., nicht?** But note that the initial comma is essential, otherwise the sentence becomes negative.

Most casual of all is **..., ne?**

Regional variants include **..., woll?** and **..., gell?**

If you're less certain about the initial statement, **..., oder?** ("or?") can be used, especially with negative sentences. However, this is far less common.

Wir zahlen doch nicht, nicht wahr?
We're not going to pay, right?

Wir zahlen doch nicht, oder?
We're not going to pay, or are we?

VOCABULARY

der	**Arzt** (¨e) /	doctor
die	**Ärztin** (-nen)	
	zum ersten Mal	for the first time
	jahrelang	for years
	plötzlich	suddenly
	unangenehm	unpleasant
der	**Schmerz** (-en)	pain
das	**Handgelenk** (-e)	wrist
	bemerken (I)	to notice
das	**Gelenk** (-e)	joint (e.g., wrist)
	steif	stiff
die	**Gelegenheit** (-en)	occasion
	passieren	to happen
der	**Schwager** (-) /	brother-in-law/
die	**Schwägerin** (-nen)	sister-in-law
der	**Umzug** (¨e)	removal
	meinen	to say (give an opinion)
der	**Beruf** (-e)	job
	benutzen (I)	to use
der	**Maurer** (-) /	bricklayer
die	**Maurerin** (-nen)	
	etwa	approximately; perhaps
der	**Fliesenleger** (-) /	tiler
die	**Fliesenlegerin** (-nen)	
	schon mal	ever
	von selbst	by itself
	röntgen	to X-ray
	wie gesagt	as (I) said
	erst mal	first of all
	untersuchen (I)	to examine
	allgemein	generally
das	**Herz** (-en)	heart
	abhören (II)	to check (heart, lungs)
der	**Blutdruck**	blood pressure
	messen	to measure
die	**Blutprobe** (-n)	blood test
	behandeln (I)	to treat
	überweisen (I)	to transfer, to hand over
	schütteln	to shake

9

A doctor receives a new patient

PATIENT Guten Tag, Frau Doktor!
ÄRZTIN Guten Tag, Sie sind zum ersten Mal bei mir, nicht?
PATIENT Ja, ich bin jahrelang bei keinem Arzt gewesen.
ÄRZTIN Und was haben Sie denn jetzt so plötzlich?
PATIENT Vor einigen Tagen habe ich sehr unangenehme Schmerzen im rechten Handgelenk bemerkt, und das Gelenk ist auch ganz steif geworden.
ÄRZTIN Bei welcher Gelegenheit ist das passiert?
PATIENT Ich habe neulich meiner Schwester und meinem Schwager beim Umzug geholfen und sehr schwere Sachen getragen. Sofort danach habe ich es gemerkt. Die haben gemeint, ich soll zum Arzt gehen.
ÄRZTIN Haben Sie einen manuellen Beruf? … mit anderen Worten, benutzen Sie Ihre Hände viel?
PATIENT Früher bin ich Maurer gewesen, aber seit etwa einem Jahr bin ich Fliesenleger.
ÄRZTIN Spielen Sie etwa Handball oder Tennis?
PATIENT Ja, ab und zu beides.
ÄRZTIN Haben Sie schon mal Probleme mit dem Handgelenk gehabt?
PATIENT Ja, vor etwa zwei Monaten, aber es ist von selbst besser geworden. Diesmal sind die Schmerzen viel stärker als vor zwei Monaten.
ÄRZTIN Hat man Ihnen das Handgelenk je geröntgt?
PATIENT Nein, wie gesagt, ich bin lange nicht mehr zum Arzt gegangen.

9

ÄRZTIN	**Ich werde Sie erst mal allgemein untersuchen ... Herz abhören ... Blutdruck messen ... Urin untersuchen ... eine Blutprobe machen ...**
PATIENT	**Warum denn das alles?**
ÄRZTIN	**Sie waren doch so lange nicht beim Arzt... und dann das Handgelenk röntgen...**
PATIENT	**... und dann werden Sie das Handgelenk behandeln, nicht?**
ÄRZTIN	**O nein! Dann überweise ich Sie an meinen Kollegen Henschel. Der ist Orthopäde!**
PATIENT	**[Schüttelt den Kopf]**

TRANSLATION

PATIENT	Hello, doctor.
DOCTOR	Hello. This is the first time you've come to see me, isn't it?
PATIENT	Yes, I haven't been to a doctor for years.
DOCTOR	And what's the matter with you now all of a sudden?
PATIENT	A few days ago I noticed some very unpleasant pains in my right wrist, and the joint also got quite stiff.
DOCTOR	On what occasion did that happen?
PATIENT	I was helping my sister and brother-in-law move (lit. "with the house-moving") recently and carrying very heavy things. I noticed it immediately afterward. They said I should go to the doctor.
DOCTOR	Do you have a manual job? ... in other words, do you use your hands a lot?
PATIENT	I used to be a bricklayer, but I've been a tiler for about a year.
DOCTOR	Do you play, say, handball or tennis?
PATIENT	Yes, both now and again.

9

DOCTOR   Have you ever had problems with your
          wrist before?
PATIENT   Yes, about two months ago, but it got better
          by itself. This time the pains are much worse
          than two months ago.
DOCTOR   Has your wrist ever been X-rayed?
PATIENT   No. As I said, I haven't been to the doctor for
          a long time.
DOCTOR   First I'll give you a general examination …
          check your heart … measure your blood
          pressure … check your urine … do a blood
          test …
PATIENT   Why all that?
DOCTOR   Well, as you haven't been to a doctor for such a
          long time … and then X-ray your wrist …
PATIENT   … and then you'll give me some treatment for
          my wrist, won't you?
DOCTOR   Oh no! Then I'll transfer you to my colleague
          Dr. Henschel. He specializes in orthopedics!
PATIENT   [Shakes his head]

Week 10

- the genitive case (used to indicate possession) and a group of masculine nouns with unusual case endings
- more separable-prefix verbs
- verb constructions with **zu** + infinitive, **um … zu, ohne … zu**, and **statt … zu**
- the passive voice
- the present perfect of modal and other auxiliary verbs
- the simple past of **haben, sein,** and modal verbs

10.1 THE GENITIVE CASE (POSSESSION)

In addition to the nominative (subject), accusative (DO), and dative (IO), there is a remaining fourth case: the genitive. This is used to indicate possession or a close relationship between two things.

In English, there are two ways of linking two nouns to show that one possesses or is related to the other:

(A) apostrophe + s
Friday's meeting
John's wife's aunt
both companies' profits
women's rights

(B) the preposition "of"
the tip of the iceberg
the opinion of the judge
the end of the matter
the brother of the deceased

In German, possession is expressed by case endings. This means that there are distinctive forms of **der**, **ein**, etc., of adjectives, and—for singular masculine and neuter nouns only—of the noun itself.

The construction is similar to (B), but look what happens to "my friend":
die Schwägerin meines Freundes
my friend's sister-in-law ("the sister-in-law of my friend")

10

Here are some other examples:

die Ansichten beider Rechtsanwälte
the views of both lawyers
der Ruf des ehemaligen Politikers
the former politician's reputation
der Wagen einer alten Dame
an old lady's car

The table below shows the declensions for the genitive case for the articles, demonstrative and possessive adjectives, etc.:

	singular			plural
	m.	f.	n.	m. f. n.
der, etc.	**des**	**der**	**des**	**der**
ein, etc.	**(k)eines**	**(k)einer**	**(k)eines**	**keiner**
diese, etc.	**dieses**	**dieser**	**dieses**	**dieser**
	jedes	**jeder**	**jedes**	**–**
poss. adj.	**unseres**	**unserer**	**unseres**	**unserer**
(e.g., **mein**)	**Ihres**	**Ihrer**	**Ihres**	**Ihrer**

In addition to the above, the following words also decline:

• an adjective after
der, etc.   adds **-en** (m. f. n. sing. & pl.)

• an adjective after
ein, etc.   adds **-en** (m. f. n. sing. & pl.)

• an adjective alone (no article) adds (m. f. n. sing. & pl.):
              -en   **-er**   **-en**   **-er**

• a masculine or neuter singular noun adds:
              -(e)s   **–**   **-(e)s**   **–**

The (**e**) of the m. and n. singular noun ending is often inserted after monosyllabic noun stems, e.g., **Freundes** friend's (compare to **Politikers** politician's).

10.2 PREPOSITIONS REQUIRING THE GENITIVE

As we saw in section 6.1, certain prepositions require that the following noun or pronoun be in a particular case. Listed below are a few common prepositions that take the genitive case. The English translations all contain "of," showing that they indicate the relationship of the following noun with something:

außerhalb	outside of
innerhalb	inside of
jenseits	on the far side of (beyond)
statt	instead of
trotz	in spite of
während	in the course of (during)
wegen	because of, on account of

There are also certain pronouns that are used with prepositions that require this case. The below are the most common—note that the pronoun combines with the preposition in these unusual forms:

stattdessen	instead (of it)
trotzdem	in spite of this, nevertheless
währenddessen	in the course of it/this
deswegen	because of this, consequently
meinetwegen	on my account, as far as I'm concerned
unseretwegen	on our account
deinetwegen	on your account

Colloquially, **wegen** can also be followed by pronouns in the dative (IO) rather than the genitive:

wegen mir	because of me
wegen uns	because of us
wegen dir	because of you
wegen ihm	because of him

10

As we just learned, most singular masculine and neuter nouns add **-(e)s** in the genitive. However, there is a group of masculine nouns that don't follow this rule. These nouns add **-(e)n** in all cases, singular and plural, except in the nominative singular, which is the form given below:

der Automat	vending machine	(and other "imported" nouns ending in **-at**)
der Bauer	farmer	
der Franzose	Frenchman	(and other nationality designations ending in **-e**, e.g., **der Pole**, but NOT **der Deutsche**, which follows different rules; see section 11.2)
der Held	hero	
der Herr	Mr., gentleman	(adds **-n** in the singular, and **-en** in the plural)
der Junge	boy	(the colloquial plural adds **-ns** throughout)
der Kollege	colleague	
der Kunde	customer	
der Mensch	person, human being, (plural) people	
der Nachbar	neighbor	
der Präsident	president	(and many other "imported" nouns ending in **-ent**)
der Soldat	soldier	(see **Automat**)
der Student	student	(see **Präsident**)
der Tourist	tourist	(and other "imported" nouns ending in **-ist**)

Many other nouns, particularly loanwords from other languages, follow the same pattern. These nouns are noted in the mini-dictionary, not by the usual information on the plural but by (**-n** noun) or (**-en** noun): e.g., **der Tourist** (**-en** noun) tourist.

10

Note that a small group of masculine **n**-nouns ending in
-e add **-ns** for the singular genitive (and **-n** in all other
cases). Here, they are in the nominative singular:

der	**Buchstabe**	letter (of the alphabet)
der	**Gedanke**	thought
der	**Glaube**	belief
der	**Name**	name
der	**Wille**	will (determination)

These are marked in the mini-dictionary with (**-ns** noun).

10.4 MORE ON SEPARABLE-PREFIX VERBS

These verbs have a prefix that can be detached from the
verb stem in different verb forms. For example, in the
past participle, the **ge-** is inserted between the separable
prefix and the stem: e.g., **ausgegangen** (went out, gone
out) (see section 9.7).

The same principle applies if the infinitive is preceded by
zu (to). This is also inserted between the prefix and the
stem: e.g., **auszugehen** (to go out). In both cases, the
verb form is spoken and written as one word.

When a separable-prefix verb is conjugated, the stem
stays in the second position, and the prefix detaches and
moves to the end of the sentence:

Ich lade meine Freunde für Sonnabend ein. (einladen)
I'm inviting my friends for Saturday.
**Er schlägt ein kaltes Mittagessen mit Brot, Käse
und Wein vor. (vorschlagen)**
He suggests a cold lunch with bread, cheese, and wine.
**Ich helfe bei den Vorbereitungen für die Konferenz
nicht mit. (mithelfen)**
I'm not helping with the preparations for the conference.

Note that **nicht**, which usually comes near the end of a
sentence, must come before the separated prefix.

10

In contrast, inseparable-prefix verbs always remain intact:

Ich empfinde gar kein Mitleid mit dieser Frau. (emp<u>find</u>en)
I feel no sympathy at all with this woman.

10.5 ZU + INFINITIVE

If a simple sentence contains both a conjugated verb and an infinitive (**-en** form), the infinitive stands right at the end of the sentence (see section 8.1):

Ich gehe zweimal in der Woche schwimmen.

Often, the infinitive is preceded by **zu** (to), just as in English. In this case, both come at the end of the sentence.

Nothing can come between **zu** and the infinitive. This is why the **zu** is inserted between the prefix and the verb stem in separable-prefix verbs.

Er hofft, morgen zu kommen.
He hopes to come tomorrow.
Wir versuchen, ein neues Haus zu finden.
We are trying to find a new house.
Ich habe vor, meine Freunde für Sonnabend einzuladen.
I intend to invite my friends for Saturday.

Here are some more complex examples:

(1) (a) **Er wird immer zögern,**   **mir seine Sorgen zu erzählen.**
He will always hesitate   to tell me his worries.

(b) **Ich habe neulich versucht,**   **den Chef für Montag einzuladen.**
I recently tried   to invite the boss for Monday.

(2) (a) **Ich werde meinen Freund bitten,** **uns ein Picknick vorzubereiten.**

I'll ask my boyfriend to make a picnic for us.

(b) **Der Arzt hat mich überredet,** **wegen des Handgelenks zum Orthopäden zu gehen.**

The doctor persuaded me to go to the orthopedic specialist with my wrist.

Sentences (1b) and (2a) show how a separable verb allows **zu** to slip between the prefix and verb stem.

Notice how each of these sentences divides into two clear parts. Each part has to remain separate—nothing from one part can stray into the other. In keeping with the rules of word order, the past participle or infinitive has to come last in each respective part.

In the sentences in (1), the subject in the first part—**er** in (a) and **ich** in (b)—is also the implied subject of the second part:

er – zögern – erzählen
ich – versuchen – einladen

This is not the case in the sentences in (2), however, where the implied subject in the second part is the direct object of the first part:

first part
(a) **ich** (SU) – **bitten** – **meinen Freund** (DO)
(b) **der Arzt** (SU) – **überreden** – **ich** (DO)

second part
(a) **meinen Freund** (implied SU) – **vorbereiten**
(b) **ich** (implied SU) – **gehen**

10

Exercise 1

◀×

Complete the following by filling each double gap with the correct separable-prefix verb from the column on the right. The short gap in each case is for the separable prefix, the longer gap for the rest of the verb.

Ich … , eine Party zu geben.	anrufen
Wir sind so viele, also … ich meine	einladen
Wohnung anders … . Ich … nur	einrichten
meine besten Freunde … , aber wir	mithelfen
sind fünfzig. Diesmal … meine	vorhaben
Freunde mal nicht … . Ich will alles	vorschlagen
alleine machen. Um 8 Uhr … ich	
sie … . Dann können sie kommen.	
Aber was sagen meine Freunde, sie …	
stattdessen … , gar nicht zu essen,	
sondern den ganzen Abend lang zu tanzen.	

10.6 EXPRESSING PURPOSE

In sentences in which the first part makes a statement and the second part explains why, in English we would use "in order to," "so as to," or simply "to." The equivalent in German is **um**, which is placed at the beginning of the second part of the sentence. Here are some examples based on the sentences from the previous section:

Er wird mich morgen besuchen,

He will visit me tomorrow

um mir seine Sorgen zu erzählen.

(in order) to tell me his worries.

Ich bin zur Chefsekretärin gegangen,

I've been to the director's personal assistant

um den Chef für Montag einzuladen.

(in order) to invite the boss for Monday.

Ich werde etwas Aufschnitt kaufen,

I'm going to buy some sliced meat

um uns ein Picknick vorzubereiten.

(so as) to prepare a picnic for us.

10

Ich muss besonders früh aufstehen,	**um wegen des Handgelenks zum Orthopäden zu gehen.**
I have to get up particularly early	(so as) to go to the orthopedic specialist for my wrist.

While it's frequent in English to just use "to" in this context, the term **um** is essential in German if the second part of the sentence gives the reason for the first.

In sentences with **um**, the implied subject of the second part of the sentence must be the same as in the first part. The two parts can also be switched around:

Um den Chef für Montag einzuladen,	**bin ich zur Chef-sekretärin gegangen.**
Um mir seine Sorgen zu erzählen,	**wird er mich morgen besuchen.**

When the order is reversed, the former second part, now first, affects the word order. As we saw in section 7.6, the verb must come second in a sentence, whatever element comes first. The whole phrase starting with **um** counts as one element, so the verb (**bin** and **wird** in the examples above) comes next, followed by the subject (**ich** and **er**).

10.7 OHNE AND STATT

Like **um**, the terms **ohne** (without) and **statt** (instead of) can be used to start the second part of a sentence to provide more information. And like **um**, sentences with **ohne** and **statt** must have the same subject in both parts, and the sequence of the parts can be reversed.

Ich kann kein Picknick vorbereiten,	**ohne etwas Aufschnitt zu kaufen.**
I can't prepare a picnic	without buying some sliced meat.

Er wird mich morgen besuchen,
He's going to visit me tomorrow

statt mir seine Sorgen am Telefon zu erzählen.
instead of telling me his worries on the telephone.

Exercise 2

1 Die Dame geht in die Stadt.
Sie kauft ein.

Die Dame geht in die Stadt, um einzukaufen.

The following pairs of sentences make up a story. Link the two sentences in each pair with **um ... zu, ohne ... zu,** or **statt ... zu**, as in the example above.

2 Anja steht früh auf.
Sie geht mit ihrem Hund spazieren.

3 Mittags kommt sie nach Hause und arbeitet im Garten.
Sie isst nicht.

4 Am Nachmittag geht sie ins Kino.
Sie fragt niemanden. (niemand = no one /
jemand = anyone, someone)

5 Sie sieht gerne Filme.
Sie kommt auf andere Gedanken.

6 Am Abend kommt ihr Freund.
Er will sie ins Restaurant einladen.

7 Sie verlässt das Restaurant während des Essens.
Sie bezahlt nicht.

8 Er bleibt im Restaurant sitzen und isst beide Portionen.
Er folgt nicht seiner Freundin.
(folgen = to follow)

10

In an active sentence, the subject performs the action of the verb. In the passive voice, the action is performed on the subject. For example:

Active: My father is showing the plans.
Passive: The plans are being shown.

The passive is useful if there is no need to draw particular attention to who or what is performing the action or if this is unknown.

In German, the passive is formed with a conjugated form of the verb **werden** + past participle. Below are some examples in the present:

Die Pläne werden von meinem Vater gezeigt.
The plans are being shown by my father. (note how the agent of the action is introduced by **von**, "by").

Jetzt werden die Pläne gezeigt.
The plans are now being shown. (who is showing the plans is not important)

Das Haus wird in diesen Tagen eingerichtet.
The house is being furnished at present.

Ich werde oft mitten in der Nacht angerufen.
I'm often called in the middle of the night.

10

One way the passive in German differs from English is that it uses **werden** (to become) as the auxiliary verb rather than **sein** (to be). It also differs in the following two respects:

(1) In English, in the passive voice, the direct object or the recipient of the action of the verb (the indirect object) becomes the subject of the sentence:
The slides are being shown.
(In the active voice, "the slides" would be a direct object— here, they are the subject.)

The guest is being shown the slides.
(In the active voice, "the guest" would be an indirect object—the recipient of the slides—here, this becomes the subject.)

But in German, the indirect object in a passive sentence cannot become the subject. While a word sequence similar to English is possible, the noun or pronoun must stay in the dative case (IO):

Dem Gast werden die Dias gezeigt.

Even with this word order, the subject remains what would be the direct object in the active sentence, i.e., **die Dias**, as can be seen from the plural verb **werden**.

(2) In German, the passive voice can be formed with verbs without a direct object. It can even be formed without a subject (or with the impersonal **es** as the subject, making it similar to the general "there is"):

    Heute Abend wird gesungen.
or **Es wird heute Abend gesungen.**
    There's some singing this evening.

    Jetzt wird schnell gegessen!
or **Es wird jetzt schnell gegessen!**
    Now it's time to eat quickly!

This means that sentences such as:
The children are now being forgiven.
The students are being helped a lot.

containing verbs that take the dative case in German (see section 4.5) must be translated as follows:

    Den Kindern wird jetzt verziehen.
or **Es wird den Kindern jetzt verziehen.**

    Den Studenten wird sehr geholfen.
or **Es wird den Studenten sehr geholfen.**

Note that when the passive refers to the future, because both the future tense and the passive are formed with **werden**, this is not normally used twice:

Wir werden nächste Woche in Französisch geprüft (werden).
We're going to be tested in French next week.

10.9 THE PRESENT PERFECT WITH MODAL VERBS

We've seen the construction of sentences with a modal verb as the auxiliary:

Ich muss den Nachbarn helfen.
I have to help the neighbors.

So if the action took place in the past, how would this be turned into the present perfect? In this case, rather than becoming a past participle, the infinitive of the auxiliary verb is used:

Ich habe den Nachbarn helfen müssen.
I have had to help the neighbors.

The infinitive of the auxiliary stands at the end of the sentence, after the infinitive of the main verb (here, **helfen**). The same applies to the other modal verbs: **dürfen, können, mögen, sollen, wollen**, and **lassen**.

Ich habe meinen Wagen waschen lassen.
I got my car washed.

However, note that all of these verbs have a past participle that is used when they are not auxiliaries: i.e., when they are used alone, without another verb (see B).

A: Kannst du geduldig warten?
Are you able to wait patiently?
B: Nein, das habe ich nie gekonnt.
No, I've never been able to (do) that.

Wir haben unser Gepäck am Bahnhof gelassen.
We have left our luggage at the station.

These "independent" past participles begin with **ge-** and (except **lassen**) end with **-t**: **gedurft, gekonnt, gemocht, gemusst, gesollt, gewollt**, and **gelassen**.

When **werden** is used as an auxiliary in the passive present perfect, the past participle is simply **worden**, but its independent past participle ("become") is **geworden**:

Die Dias sind von meinem Vater gezeigt worden.
The slides were shown by my father.
Die Kunden sind heutzutage sehr frech geworden.
Customers have become very bold these days.

10.10 THE SIMPLE PAST TENSE

As we've seen, Germans are most likely to use the present perfect to refer to any event in the past in everyday conversation.

However, there is a simple (single word) past tense as well, which is used more frequently for the verb **sein** as well as **haben**, which avoids having two forms of the same verb in one sentence necessitated by the present perfect (e.g., **er ist ... gewesen; ich habe ... gehabt**).

The simple past is also often preferred for other auxiliary verbs, as it reduces the number of verbs required in the sentence to two. Compare the following:

present perfect	simple past
Ich bin vier Wochen krank gewesen.	**Ich war vier Wochen krank.**

    I have been/was ill for four weeks.

Wir haben viel Pech gehabt.	**Wir hatten viel Pech.**

    We have had/had very bad luck.

Ich habe den Nachbarn helfen müssen. **Ich musste den Nachbarn helfen.**
I have had/had to help the neighbors.

Die Dias sind von meinem Vater gezeigt worden. **Die Dias wurden von meinem Vater gezeigt.**
The slides have been/were shown by my father.

Here is the simple past of **haben**, **sein**, the modal verbs and the auxiliary **werden**:

	haben	**sein**
ich/er/sie(she)**/es**	**hatte**	**war**
du (you, inf. sing.)	**hattest**	**warst**
wir/Sie/sie(they)	**hatten**	**waren**
ihr (you, inf. pl.)	**hattet**	**wart**

	dürfen	**können**
ich/er/sie(she)**/es**	**durfte**	**konnte**
du	**durftest**	**konntest**
wir/Sie/sie(they)	**durften**	**konnten**
ihr	**durftet**	**konntet**

	mögen	**müssen**
ich/er/sie(she)**/es**	**mochte**	**musste**
du	**mochtest**	**musstest**
wir/Sie/sie(they)	**mochten**	**mussten**
ihr	**mochtet**	**musstet**

	sollen	**wollen**
ich/er/sie(she)**/es**	**sollte**	**wollte**
du	**solltest**	**wolltest**
wir/Sie/sie(they)	**sollten**	**wollten**
ihr	**solltet**	**wolltet**

	lassen	**werden**
ich/er/sie(she)**/es**	**ließ**	**wurde**
du	**ließest**	**wurdest**
wir/Sie/sie(they)	**ließen**	**wurden**
ihr	**ließet**	**wurdet**

10

Note that the first- and third-person singular forms are the same in this tense. Hence, the third-person singular never ends in **-t**, unlike in the present tense.

The conjugation follows three patterns, plus **werden**, which conjugates in a unique way. Two of these are significant for learning German past tenses in general (see section 12.1), while a third is typical of another small group. The four conjugation types are:

1 sein, lassen
The stem changes (**war, ließ**) and is used without any ending.

2 sollen, wollen
The stem stays the same and is followed by **-t-** and the ending **-e**.

3 haben, dürfen, können, mögen müssen
The stem changes (**hat-, durf-, konn-, moch-, muss-**) and is followed by **-t-** and the ending **-e**.

4 werden
The stem vowel (**wurd-**) changes and is followed by the ending **-e**.

Pattern **1** is followed by the many German verbs that change stem in the simple past tense (like the English "come/came"). We'll call these "new-stem verbs."

Pattern **2** is the model for most verbs, which simply add **-t-** to the verb stem, followed by an ending. These are "same-stem verbs" (like the English "rush/rushed").

Pattern **3** is a mixture of **1** and **2**: the stem changes, plus **-t-** is added, always followed by an ending. These conjugations are somewhat akin to the English "kneel/knelt" or "buy/bought."

10

VOCABULARY

Some new words for the following conversation:

der	**Freund (-e) /**	boyfriend/
	die Freundin (-nen)	girlfriend
die	**Silvesterfahrt (-en)**	New Year's Eve trip
der	**Winterprospekt (-e)**	winter brochure
	anbieten (II)	to offer
	preiswert	reasonably priced
das	**Allgäu**	mountainous area in Southern Bavaria
der	**Preis (-e)**	price
	reichhaltig	varied
der	**Ausflug (¨-e)**	excursion
die	**Abendveranstaltung (-en)**	evening entertainment, event
das	**Neujahrsfrühstück (-e)**	New Year's Day breakfast
der	**Sonderpreis (-e)**	special price
die	**Unterkunft (¨e)**	accommodation
das	**Doppelzimmer (-)**	double room
das	**Einzelzimmer (-)**	single room
das	**Silvesterfestessen (-)**	New Year's Eve banquet
die	**Skimöglichkeit (-en)**	opportunity for skiing
	sorgen für	to see to
die	**Übernachtung (-en)**	overnight stay
	hin und zurück	there and back, i.e., return journey
der	**Hinweg (-e)**	outward journey
die	**Rückfahrt (-en)**	return journey
das	**Gleiche**	the same
	unterwegs	on the way
	genügend	sufficiently
	anhalten (II)	to stop, to pull up
	jeweils	each time
	einnehmen (II)	to eat, to take, to consume

10

die	Erfrischung (-en)	refreshment
der	Gasthof (¨e)	inn
der	Löwe (-n noun)	lion
	unterbringen (II)	to accommodate
der	Grundpreis (-e)	basic price
	enthalten (I)	to contain, to include
die	Dusche (-n)	shower
der	Zuschlag (¨e)	additional charge
	nicht in Frage kommen	to be out of the question
die	Veranstaltung (-en)	event (entertainment)
	einbegriffen	included
der	Geschmack (¨e)	taste
	tagsüber	during the daytime
	gesellig	sociable
das	Beisammensein	being with other people
der	Gesellschaftsraum (¨e)	lounge
	genießen (I)	to enjoy
die	Möglichkeit (-en)	opportunity
das	Skifahren	skiing
das	Festessen (-)	banquet
	tanzen	to dance
der	Tanz (¨e)	dance
	veranstalten (I)	to arrange, to put on
	nach Wunsch	as required, to order
das	Feuerwerk	fireworks
	loslassen (II)	to set off
das	Sektfrühstück	champagne breakfast
	klingen	to sound
	beschränken (I)	to limit
	anstrengend	energetic, strenuous
der	Teilnehmer (-) / die Teilnehmerin (-nen)	participant
die	Leute	people
das	Gegenteil	opposite
die	Gruppe (-n)	group
die	goldene Hochzeit (-en)	golden anniversary
	feiern	to celebrate
	besprechen (I)	to discuss, talk over

10

Inquiring at a bus tour company about a short New Year vacation

JUNGER MANN Meine Freundin und ich sind daran interessiert, eine Silvesterfahrt zu machen.

BERATERIN Gut, ich zeige Ihnen unseren Winterprospekt. Wir bieten dieses Jahr eine sehr preiswerte Fahrt mit Luxusbus nach Oberstdorf im Allgäu an, sieben Tage vom 28. Dezember bis zum 3. Januar inklusive.

JUNGER MANN [Liest aus dem Winterprospekt]

---

7 Tage Silvesterfahrt mit Luxusbus ins Allgäu

5 Nächte in Oberstdorf

reichhaltiges Programm mit Ausflügen, Abendveranstaltungen und Neujahrssektfrühstück

Sonderpreis €790,–

Unterkunft in Doppelzimmern Einzelzimmer €30,– extra Silvesterfestessen €85,– extra Skimöglichkeiten

---

JUNGER MANN Was wird da alles für den Preis angeboten?

BERATERIN Ja, da ist erst mal die Fahrt hin und zurück im Luxusbus. Für alles wird gesorgt ... eine Übernachtung in einem netten Hotel auf dem Hinweg und das Gleiche auf der Rückfahrt ...

JUNGER MANN Wie wird unterwegs gegessen?

BERATERIN Es wird natürlich genügend oft angehalten, und das Mittagessen wird

10

jeweils während einer längeren Pause in einem Gasthof eingenommen. Andere Erfrischungen werden im Bus serviert ... Ja, und in Oberstdorf selbst wird man im Gasthof Zum Löwen untergebracht. Der Grundpreis enthält die Unterbringung in Doppelzimmern mit Dusche und Toilette, aber es werden auch Einzelzimmer angeboten für einen Zuschlag von €30,–. Aber das kommt für Sie wohl nicht in Frage ...?

JUNGER MANN Was für Veranstaltungen sind im Preis einbegriffen?

BERATERIN Für jeden Geschmack wird gesorgt ... Tagsüber werden drei kleinere Ausflüge gemacht, und jeden Abend wird getanzt, oder man kann das gesellige Beisammensein in der Bar oder im Gesellschaftsraum genießen. Es gibt auch Möglichkeiten zum Skifahren, aber das muss extra bezahlt werden.

JUNGER MANN Und zu Silvester und am Neujahrstag selbst ...?

BERATERIN Silvester gibt es Tanz, und um elf Uhr wird eine besondere Show veranstaltet. Silvester wird auch um acht Uhr ein Festessen nach Wunsch serviert für einen Zuschlag von €85,–. Um Mitternacht wird dann das Feuerwerk losgelassen. Am 1. Januar wird ab neun Uhr ein Sektfrühstück eingenommen.

JUNGER MANN Das klingt alles sehr schön. Und sind noch Plätze frei?

BERATERIN Ja, wir haben noch sechs Plätze frei. Wir mussten die Zahl der Teilnehmer wegen der Größe unseres Busses auf dreißig beschränken.

JUNGER MANN Bei solch einem anstrengenden Programm sind die anderen Teilnehmer doch bestimmt alles junge Leute ...

10

BERATERIN	**O nein, ganz im Gegenteil! Sechzehn der Teilnehmer fahren als Gruppe, um Silvester eine goldene Hochzeit zu feiern.**
JUNGER MANN	**Oh! Das muss ich doch noch mal mit meiner Freundin besprechen ...**

TRANSLATION

YOUNG MAN	My girlfriend and I are interested in doing a New Year's Eve trip.
ADVISOR	Right, I'll show you our winter brochure. This year, we're offering a very reasonable trip by luxury bus to Oberstdorf in the Allgäu, seven days from December 28 to January 3 inclusive.
YOUNG MAN	[Reads from the winter brochure]

7-day New Year's Eve trip
to the Allgäu by luxury bus

5 nights in Oberstdorf

Varied program with excursions,
evening entertainment, and
New Year's Day champagne breakfast

Special price €790,–

Accommodation in double rooms
Single room €30,– extra
New Year's Eve banquet €85,– extra
Opportunities for skiing

YOUNG MAN	What sort of things do you get for the price?
ADVISOR	Well, first of all there's the outward and return journey in a luxury bus. Everything is taken care of ... an overnight stop in a nice hotel on the way out and the same on the return journey ...
YOUNG MAN	How are the meals provided on the journey?

10

ADVISOR   There are plenty of stops, of course, and there is a fairly long break for lunch at a hotel. Other refreshments are served in the bus … and in Oberstdorf itself you stay in the Lion Inn. The basic price includes accommodation in double rooms with shower and toilet, but single rooms are also available at an extra charge of €30. But you wouldn't be interested in that, I suppose …?

YOUNG MAN   What sort of entertainment is included in the price?

ADVISOR   Every taste is catered to … In the daytime there are three shortish excursions, and there's dancing every evening, or you can socialize in the bar or the lounge. There are also opportunities to ski, but you have to pay extra for that.

YOUNG MAN   And on New Year's Eve and New Year's Day themselves …?

ADVISOR   On New Year's Eve there's a dance, and at eleven o'clock a special show will be put on. And on New Year's Eve there will also be a banquet served to order at eight o'clock for an extra charge of €85. Then at midnight the fireworks will be set off. On January 1 from nine o'clock onward you can have a champagne breakfast.

YOUNG MAN   That all sounds very nice. And are there still spots available?

ADVISOR   Yes, we still have six spots left. We have had to restrict the number of participants to thirty because of the size of our bus.

YOUNG MAN   With such a busy program I suppose the other participants are all young people …

ADVISOR   Oh no, just the opposite! Sixteen of the participants are going as a group to celebrate a golden anniversary on New Year's Eve.

YOUNG MAN   Oh! I'll have to discuss this again with my girlfriend …

10

Week 11

- *terms for expressing quantity ("all the," "a little," "many," "another," etc.) or that something is the same*
- *adjectives used as nouns*
- *linking words that affect the word order of a subordinate clause*
- *reflexive pronouns ("myself," "yourself," etc.)*
- *reflexive verbs*

11.1 TERMS THAT EXPRESS QUANTITY

By now you'll be getting used to the fact that words used with or to replace nouns decline, as we saw with terms like **dieser** (this), **jeder** (every), **meiner** (my), etc. (sections 7.1–7.2). So, you won't be surprised to hear that terms that refer to the quantity of a noun, or its similarity to something else, also inflect.

The declensions of these terms vary not just according to gender, number, and case but also by the type of noun in terms of whether it is uncountable (e.g., "water") or countable (e.g., "shop").

The key terms are listed below in the categories that affect how they decline, with references to the sets of endings they take (set 1, set 2, or set 3 from section 7.3, or the genitive endings in section 10.1).

(a) Before any type of noun

the same (identical)	**derselbe, dieselbe, dasselbe**, etc.	Both parts of the word decline: the definite article with its usual endings, and **selb-** with set 1 endings.
the same (alike)	**der gleich**, etc.	The definite article declines, as does **gleich**, with set 1 endings.
all (of) the, the whole (of the)	**der ganz**, etc.	The definite article declines, as does **ganz**, with set 1 or 2 endings.

11

Ich bin in derselben* Gruppe wie du.
I'm in the same group as you.
Ich habe das gleiche* Kleid wie du gekauft.
I've bought the same dress as you.
Die ganze Arbeit hat er alleine geschafft.
He's managed all the work ("the entire work") on his own.
Meine ganzen Bücher sind nass geworden.
All my books got wet.
Ein ganzes Jahr hat er dafür gebraucht.
He took a whole year for it.

* In practice there is a lot of overlap between **derselbe** and **der gleich** (in their various declensions).

(b) Before uncountable nouns

little	**wenig**	No ending required.
a little	**etwas**	No ending required.
some	**einige**, etc.	Takes set 3 endings.
a bit of	**ein bisschen**	The indefinite article (**ein**) declines with its usual endings (**bisschen** is a neuter noun).
a drop of	**ein Tropfen**	The indefinite article declines with its usual endings (**Tropfen** m.).
enough	**genug** **genügend**	No ending required.
much, a lot of	**viel**	No ending required.
all (of), etc.	**der ganz**, etc.	See section (a).
all (the)	**alles**, etc.	Takes set 1 endings, but before m. and n. **n-**nouns ending in **-(e)s**, takes **-en** in the genitive.
all that/this/ my, etc.	**all der/dieser** **all mein**, etc.	has no ending, but the adjective declines.

Examples:
für wenig Geld for little money
mit etwas Salz with a little salt
vor einiger Zeit some time ago

mit einem bisschen Papier with a bit of paper
mit einem Tropfen Öl with a drop of oil
Wir haben genug Wein. We have enough wine.
bei viel Arbeit with a lot of work
bei allem guten Willen with the best will in the world
trotz allen Komforts in spite of all the comfort
wegen all der Unruhe because of all that noise

(c) Before countable nouns in the singular

the same	**derselbe**, etc.	See section (a).
any, some or other	**irgendein**	Takes the same endings as **ein**.
another (one more)	**noch ein**	**ein** declines with its usual endings.
another (a different one)	**ein ander**, etc.	**ein** declines with its usual endings, **ander** takes set 2 endings.
the whole (of the)	**der ganz**, etc.	See section (a).

Heute kommt irgendein Vertreter von der Versicherung.
Some representative or other from the insurance company is coming today.
Heute kommt noch ein Vertreter von der Versicherung.
Another (one more) representative from the insurance company is coming today.
Heute kommt ein anderer Vertreter von der Versicherung.
Another (different) representative from the insurance company is coming today.

(d) Before countable nouns in the plural

a pair of	**ein Paar**	The indefinite article declines with its usual endings (**Paar** is a neuter noun). The following noun has

		the same case.
the two	**der beiden**, etc.	The definite article declines with its usual endings, **beiden** takes set 1 endings.
both	**beide**, etc.	Takes set 3 endings.
a few	**ein paar**	No endings, though a following noun in the dative may need **-(e)n**.
some	**einige**, etc.	Takes set 3 endings.
	mehrere, etc.	Takes set 3 endings.
many	**viele**, etc.	Takes set 3 endings.
enough	**genug**	See section (b).
	genügend	
all (of) the	**alle**, etc.	Takes set 3 endings, but any following adjective adds **-en** in all cases.

Examples:

von einem Paar alten Schuhen
from an old pair of shoes
wegen der beiden Damen
because of the two ladies
mit beiden Händen
with both hands
vor ein paar Wochen
a few weeks ago

für einige gute Freunde	for some good friends
für mehrere gute Freunde	for several good friends
für viele gute Freunde	for many good friends
für alle guten Freunde	for all the good friends

11.2 USING ADJECTIVES AS NOUNS

Adjectives are often used as nouns in German. While in English this is possible, it is typically limited to denoting collective categories of people (e.g., "the rich," "the disadvantaged," "the British") and some abstract categories ("the good, the bad, the indifferent").
But in German this usage is almost unrestricted.

Here's an example from the last conversation (p.151) that works in both languages:

das Gleiche auf der Rückfahrt
the same on the return journey

Here the adjective **gleich**, given an initial capital letter, has become a neuter noun. This is the gender for all adjectival nouns that do not refer specifically to a male or a female.

Adjectival nouns take the adjective endings described in section 7.3. For instance, "a German" is **ein Deutscher** if a man, but **eine Deutsche** if a woman, because the noun is derived from the adjective **deutsch**. In the mini-dictionary, adjectival nouns are marked (adj.) to show that they require adjective endings.

Adjectival nouns can be created as needed. Many of them derive from the past participle (the -ed form) or present participle (the -ing form) of a verb (for the latter, see section 13.1). For example, the past participle **gefangen** (caught, captured) used as an adjectival noun becomes **der/die Gefangene** (the prisoner).

The present participle **überlebend** (surviving) used as a noun becomes **der/die Überlebende** (survivor).

Another common way to use adjectives as nouns is in combination with **etwas** (something) or **nichts** (nothing), e.g., "something special" or "nothing surprising." In these situations, the adjective has the endings given in section 7.3, set 3.

11

Die Stunde soll mit etwas Einfachem anfangen.
The lesson should start with something simple.
Alles war ruhig, nichts Wesentliches ist geschehen.
Everything was quiet; nothing important happened.

But with **alles** (everything), as it already has the neuter ending **-es**, an adjectival noun takes the endings indicated in section 7.3, set 1:

Ich wünsche dir alles Gute zum Geburtstag.
I wish you all the best for your birthday.
In allem Praktischen war er der Klassenbeste.
In everything practical he was the best in the class.

11.3 LINKING CLAUSES

As we've seen, a sentence can consist of different parts that give extra information about the main clause. For example, a phrase with **zu** + infinitive may be added to the main clause, or a phrase with **um** (in order to), **ohne** (without), or **statt** (instead of) followed by **zu** + infinitive.

As well as such additional phrases, there may be a subordinate clause. This is a group of words that contains a subject and a conjugated verb that is linked to a main clause.

(1) The simplest way of linking a subordinate clause to a main clause in German is just to attach them with no linking word. (However, note that in German, a comma is required in between the clauses.) This has no effect on the word order of either clause. For example:

Der Arzt sagt, ich soll nur Fisch oder mageres Fleisch essen.
The doctor says I should only eat fish or lean meat.
Die haben gemeint, ich soll zum Arzt gehen.
They said I should go to the doctor.

In both of these examples, the main clause comes first.

11

But if the order of the clauses is reversed, the word order in the main clause changes:

Ich soll nur Fisch oder mageres Fleisch essen, sagt der Arzt.

This is because the entire subordinate clause becomes the first element in the sentence, so the verb in the main clause needs to be in the second position.

(2) The scope for joining clauses is immeasurably widened by the use of linking words, or conjunctions, to introduce the subordinate clause. Here are some of the most common conjunctions:

und	and
aber	but
oder	or
sondern	but rather (on the contrary)
sondern ... auch	but ... also

These can be used to join comparable words as well as phrases, clauses, or even sentences. They function like their English equivalents and generally have no effect on the word order:

Es gibt auch Möglichkeiten zum Skifahren, aber das muss extra bezahlt werden.
There are also opportunities to ski, but you'll have to pay extra for that.

If any of these conjunctions are used to link sentences in which the word order has already been affected by some other factor (see section 11.4), the new word order is retained for the sentence attached by **und**, **aber**, etc.

Note that the general conjunction for "but" is **aber**, whereas **sondern** is used in two specific contexts:

• If the sense is "not only ... but also," the German is **nicht nur ... sondern auch**.

- If the sense is "not … but rather," the German is **nicht** (or another negative, such as **kein**) **... sondern**:

Er schickt keinen Brief, sondern er will mit mir persönlich sprechen.
He's not sending a letter but intends to speak to me personally.

(3) Another key conjunction is **denn**, whose meaning is explanatory: it can translate to "as," "since," "because," or "for." This linking word is a rule unto itself. Like the conjunctions in (2) it doesn't affect word order, but it can't link anything except sentences. The clause it introduces must come after the main clause.

Er kann mir nicht böse sein, denn er hat selbst Schuld daran.
He can't be cross with me since it's his own fault.

Today there is a clear tendency in spoken German, as opposed to written German, to use the conjunction **weil** (see section 11.4) in place of **denn**. In the same way, when it introduces a clause, it doesn't affect the word order:

Ich kann ihm nicht böse sein, weil ich habe selbst Schuld daran.
I can't be cross with him because it's my own fault.

11

(1) Relative pronouns (who, that, which, whose, etc.)

	singular			plural	
	m.	f.	n.	m. f. n.	
SU	**der**	**die**	**das**	**die**	who, which, that
DO	**den**	**die**	**das**	**die**	who(m), which, that
IO	**dem**	**der**	**dem**	**denen**	to/for whom, to/for which
poss.	**dessen**	**deren**	**dessen**	**deren**	of whom, of which, whose

The forms of the German relative pronoun are the same as the definite article (section 9.1), plus **dessen** and **deren** for the genitive case (indicated here with the abbreviation for possession). They introduce a clause that provides additional information about a noun or pronoun previously mentioned in the main clause.

The relative pronoun must agree with the gender (m., f., or n.) or number (singular or plural) of the noun it refers to, but the choice of case is determined by the grammatical function of the relative pronoun (whether it is a subject, direct or indirect object, the object of a preposition, etc.).

SU **Ich bringe meinen Sohn, der nach Berlin fährt, zum Bahnhof.**
I'm taking my son, who is going to Berlin, to the station.

Das Fleisch, das auf dem Tisch liegt, kannst du für den Hund nehmen.
You can take the meat that's on the table for the dog.

DO **Mein Chef, für den ich seit zehn Jahren arbeite, ist sehr unsympathisch.**
My boss, for whom I've been working for ten years, is very unpleasant.

11

Wir haben den Urlaub, den wir auf Zypern verbracht haben, ganz toll gefunden.
We found the vacation (that) we spent in Cyprus really fantastic.

10 **Meine Schwiegertochter, der ich gestern Blumen geschenkt habe, hat sie zum Blumengeschäft zurückgebracht.**
My daughter-in-law, to whom I gave some flowers yesterday, took them back to the florist's.

Der Verwandte, bei dem ich wohne, ist wie ein Vater zu mir.
The relative who I live with ("with whom I live") is like a father to me.

poss. **Hans, dessen Frau aus Ägypten kommt, lernt Arabisch.**
Hans, whose wife comes from Egypt, is learning Arabic.

Die Frau, deren Auto falsch geparkt ist, spricht mit dem Polizisten.
The woman whose car is illegally parked is talking to the policeman.

As seen in all these examples, the conjugated verb in the clause introduced by the relative pronoun must be placed at the end of the clause. This rule applies to all the types of clauses described in this section.

Finally, when the relative pronoun follows a preposition, and if it refers to a noun that is not a living being, the alternative **wo(r)-** can be attached in front of the preposition. (This is like **da(r)-** described in section 8.8.)

Die Fehler, über die ich gerade lache, sind eigentlich überhaupt nicht witzig.
or
Die Fehler, worüber ich gerade lache, sind eigentlich überhaupt nicht witzig.
The mistakes I'm just laughing about aren't actually funny at all.

11

(2) Subordinating conjunctions (that, whether, when, etc.)

Other words that can introduce a subordinate clause include **dass** (that), **ob** (whether), **wann** (when), **was** (what), **warum** (why), **welcher** etc. (which), **wer** (whoever), **wen** (whom), **wessen** (whose), **wem** (to whom), **wie** (as), and **wo** (where). These enable the entire clause to be the subject or direct object of the main clause:

SU **Dass wir heute Abend kein Essen im Haus haben, ist nicht meine Schuld.**
or
Es ist nicht meine Schuld, dass wir heute Abend kein Essen im Haus haben.
It's not my fault that we have no food in the house this evening.

DO **Kannst du mir sagen, ob er morgen kommt?**
Can you tell me whether he's coming tomorrow?

SU **Wann er morgen aufsteht, ist vollkommen egal.**
or
Es ist vollkommen egal, wann er morgen aufsteht.
It's completely immaterial when he gets up tomorrow.

DO **Weißt du zufällig, wessen Regenschirm hier liegt?**
Do you know by chance whose umbrella this is here?

This includes contexts where the clause may not appear to be the object of the main clause, although in fact it is, because an optional word has been omitted:

Ich bin froh (darüber), dass er endlich zu Hause ist.
I'm glad (about the fact) that he's home at last.

Here, in English "about the fact" sounds artificial, but including the optional **darüber** would sound natural in

German. This way of producing a "complete" main clause uses **da(r)-** to stand for the object of a preposition (**über**). The full object is then stated in the clause introduced by **dass.**

In situations when the preposition is essential to the meaning of an idiom, the construction with **da(r)-** in the main clause is mandatory, as in the following:

Wir sind dafür, dass das Licht ausgemacht wird.
We are for the light being switched off.
Mein Vater ist dagegen, dass ich den Führerschein mache.
My father is against me taking my driving test.

Here the sense depends entirely on **für** and **gegen**, but there are also many combinations of verb + preposition and adjective + preposition where, though the sense is clear from the verb or adjective, usage requires the preposition to be stated (and therefore **da(r)-** in the main clause). Examples include **bestehen auf** (to insist on) and **einverstanden mit** (in agreement with):

Ich bestehe darauf, dass er sofort bezahlt.
I insist on him paying immediately.
Er ist damit einverstanden, dass sie den Führerschein macht.
He's in agreement with her taking her driving test.

Nor is the **da(r)-** + preposition construction limited to contexts where the subordinate clause is introduced by **dass**. For example, the expression **abhängen von** (to depend on) is often followed by a clause introduced by **ob**, **wo**, **wie**, etc.:

Meine Entscheidung hängt davon ab, ob der Versuch gelingt.
My decision depends on whether the attempt succeeds.

By the way, do not confuse **dass** with **das**; **dass** is always a conjunction.

11

Exercise 1

Revise the following mini-story by using **dass** to introduce each subordinate clause. The first one has been done for you.

1 Martin schlägt vor, Paul soll ihm helfen.→
   Martin schlägt vor, dass Paul ihm helfen soll.

2 Paul bittet darum, Martin soll solche Vorschläge nicht machen.

3 Martin besteht darauf, Paul soll endlich mal etwas tun.

4 Paul findet die Arbeit so anstrengend, er verletzt sein Handgelenk plötzlich.

5 Jetzt hat Martin solches Mitleid, er schickt Paul zum Arzt.

6 Der Arzt sieht sofort, Paul ist einfach faul!

(3) Temporal and causal subordinating conjunctions

These fulfill the same function at the beginning of a clause as a preposition does before a noun. One or two are identical or nearly identical to the equivalent prepositions:

Bis fünf Uhr ...	(**bis** preposition)
Until five o'clock ...	
Bis er kommt, ...	(**bis** conjunction)
Until he comes ...	
Während des Konzerts ...	(**während** prep.)
During the concert ...	
Während das Orchester spielt, ...	(**während** conj.)
While the orchestra is playing ...	
Nach dem Essen ...	(**nach** preposition)
After the meal ...	
Nachdem wir gegessen haben, ...	(**nachdem** conj.)
After we have eaten ...	
Vor Weihnachten ...	(**vor** preposition)
Before Christmas ...	
Bevor wir anfangen, ...	(**bevor** conjunction)
Before we begin ...	

11

Others are more remote from the preposition with the equivalent meaning:

Wegen des schlechten Wetters ... (**wegen** preposition)
Because of the bad weather ...
Weil das Wetter schlecht ist, ... (**weil** conj.)
Because the weather is bad ...
Trotz meiner Erkältung ... (**trotz** preposition)
In spite of my cold ...
Obwohl ich erkältet bin, ... (**obwohl** conj.)
Although I have a cold ...

These conjunctions that have similar meanings to prepositions relate either to (a) time or (b) causality. Here are some of the most frequent:

(a) Time

als	when (single period or point of time in the past)
bevor	before
bis	until
nachdem	after
seitdem	since
sobald	as soon as
während	while
wenn	whenever (repeated periods or points of time in the past or present)

(b) Causal connection

da	as, since
damit	so that, in order that (purpose)
obwohl	although
ohne dass	without
so dass	so that (effect), with the result that
statt dass	instead of
während	whereas
weil	because
wenn	if
wo	seeing that

Note that **so dass** (so that) is used only where a consequence is being referred to:

Ich habe meinen Hausschlüssel verloren, so dass ich nicht ins Haus komme.
I've lost my front door key, so (that) I can't get into the house.

To convey purpose or intention, use **damit**:

Er hat das Schloss ausgetauscht, damit ich mit meinem Hausschlüssel nicht ins Haus komme.
He's changed the lock so that I can't get into the house with my front door key. (i.e., in order to prevent me)

With the terms **ohne** (without) and **statt** (instead) (see section 10.7), if the subject of the subordinate clause is different from the subject of the main clause, they need to be followed by **dass**:

Ich kann kaum anfangen zu lesen, ohne dass mich eins der Kinder stört.
I can barely start reading without one of the children disturbing me.
Meine Eltern haben mir den Englischkurs bezahlt, statt dass ich mein eigenes Geld dafür nehmen musste.
My parents paid for the English class for me instead of my having to use my own money for it.

11

Exercise 2

Rewrite the following so that each contains a clause introduced by **bevor, bis, nachdem, obwohl, während**, or **weil**, as appropriate. The first one has been done for you.

1 Vor dem Essen muss man die Hände waschen.→
  Bevor man isst, muss man die Hände waschen.

2 Nach dem Essen soll man eigentlich nicht schlafen.

3 Während des Essens darf man nicht zu viel reden.

4 Trotz des vielen Redens hat er eigentlich nicht viel gesagt.

5 Wegen des schönen Wetters müssen wir endlich im Garten arbeiten.

6 Bis zum Anfang des Programms kannst du noch schön in der Küche helfen!

7 Wegen deines hohen Blutdrucks musst du weniger arbeiten.

8 Trotz seiner starken Schmerzen läuft er jeden Tag.
  (stark = strong; der Schmerz = pain)

11.5 REFLEXIVE PRONOUNS

A reflexive pronoun refers back to the subject of the verb, e.g., "myself," "yourself," "themselves," etc.

In German, these decline in the accusative (DO) and, if there's another object, the dative (IO). Their forms are the same as the personal pronouns in these cases, except in the third-person and the formal, which are **sich**:

	DO	IO
myself	**mich**	**mir**
yourself (informal sing.)	**dich**	**dir**
himself, herself, itself, oneself	**sich**	**sich**
ourselves	**uns**	**uns**
yourselves (informal pl.)	**euch**	**euch**
themselves	**sich**	**sich**
yourself, yourselves (formal)	**sich**	**sich**

Wir kaufen uns für nächsten Sommer einen Wohnwagen. (IO)
We're buying ourselves a caravan for next summer.
Du siehst furchtbar müde aus, du musst dich mehr schonen. (DO)
You look terribly tired. You have to take it easy ("spare yourself more").

In the third person and formal, **sich** is used for both cases:

Meine Eltern haben mir den Brief nicht gegeben, sondern ihn für sich behalten. (DO)
My parents didn't give me the letter but kept it for themselves.
Mein Bruder hat sich einen neuen Sportwagen angeschafft. (IO)
My brother bought himself a new sports car.
Wenn Sie sich nicht etwas mehr schonen, machen Sie sich kaputt. (DO)
If you don't take it easier ("spare yourself a bit more") you'll wear yourself out.

(Note that in German, the pronoun in "to buy oneself" is an indirect object, in the sense "to buy for oneself.")

The plural reflexive pronouns can also mean "each other, one another":

Weil wir im selben Alter sind, haben wir uns sofort geduzt.
Because we're the same age, we addressed each other with "du" immediately.

In German, reflexive pronouns are required in all contexts where the pronoun relates to the subject of the sentence, even when English would not use a reflexive pronoun. Notice in the following examples that **sich** is used rather than **ihm** (him, dative) or **Sie** (you, accusative):

Er hat nicht genug Geld bei sich.
He doesn't have enough money on him ("himself").

Jetzt haben Sie Ihren besten Freund gegen sich.
Now you have your best friend against you ("yourself").

Lastly, the German equivalent of the English "myself," etc., used to emphasize a point is **selbst**:

Probier diesen Kuchen, ich habe ihn selbst gemacht.
Try this cake—I made it myself.

11.6 REFLEXIVE VERBS

Certain verbs in German are always used with a reflexive pronoun. Some of these correspond to verbs in English:

Er hat sich verletzt und muss zum Arzt (gehen).
He hurt himself and has to go to the doctor.

However, reflexive verbs are far more common in German, so there are a number of verbs that require a reflexive pronoun where you would not expect one in English. Let's look at some of these.

(1) The equivalent of "to get" + past participle in English is conveyed by a reflexive verb, such as:

to get annoyed	**sich ärgern**
to get dressed	**sich anziehen (II)**
to get drunk	**sich betrinken (I)**
to get excited	**sich aufregen (II)**
to get lost	**sich verirren (I)**
	sich verlaufen (I)
to get ready	**sich vorbereiten (II)**
to get undressed	**sich ausziehen (II)**
to get used/accustomed (to)	**sich gewöhnen (an) (I)**

As well as situations of getting oneself ready, such as:

to shave	**sich rasieren**
to wash	**sich waschen**

In a clause where the verb comes last, the reflexive pronoun can come immediately after the conjunction, even before the subject noun to which it relates.

Während sich mein Bruder wäscht (*or* mein Bruder sich wäscht), ziehe ich mich an.
While my brother's washing, I'll get dressed.

However, if the subject of the clause is itself a pronoun, it must precede the reflexive pronoun:

Während er sich wäscht, ziehe ich mich an.
While he's washing, I'll get dressed.

(2) The equivalent of "to be" + past participle (or an adjective with a similar meaning), where the verb often describes a state of mind. Some common examples include:

to be ashamed	**sich schämen**
to be embarrassed	**sich genieren**
to be frightened (of)	**sich fürchten (vor)**
to be interested (in)	**sich interessieren (für)**
to be pleased (at)	**sich freuen (über)**
to be surprised	**sich wundern**

Er bittet seine Mutter nicht um Geld, weil er sich geniert.
He doesn't ask his mother for money because he's embarrassed.

Er findet die Ferien langweilig, denn er interessiert sich für nichts.
He finds the holidays boring, since he's not interested in anything.

Ich gratuliere, ich freue mich sehr über Ihren Erfolg.
I congratulate (you). I'm very pleased at your success.

Ich wundere mich, dass du bei so schönem Wetter im Haus bleibst.
I'm surprised that you're staying inside the house in such lovely weather.

11

(3) A number of verbs that are more difficult to categorize, but some of which refer to mental states or actions related to feelings, etc.:

to apologize	**sich entschuldigen (I)**
to approach	**sich nähern**
to be, to be located	**sich befinden (I)**
to catch a cold	**sich erkälten (I)**
to complain	**sich beklagen (I)**
to feel (e.g., sad)	**sich fühlen**
to hurry	**sich beeilen (I)**
to imagine (surmise)	**sich (IO) einbilden (II)**
(envision)	**sich (IO) vorstellen (II)**
to long (for)	**sich sehnen (nach)**
to look forward (to)	**sich freuen (auf)**
to remember	**sich erinnern (an) (I)**
to say thank you, to express one's thanks	**sich bedanken (I)**

Der Junge ist noch so klein, ich habe ihn mir größer vorgestellt.
The boy is still so small. I imagined him taller.
Ich habe Hunger, ich freue mich sehr auf das Essen.
I'm hungry. I'm really looking forward to the meal (literally, "to the food").

(4) Some ideas are conveyed in German by impersonal reflexive phrases with the subject **es**, for example:

to be, to be about, to be a matter of	**sich handeln um**

Ich muss Sie leider stören, es handelt sich um Ihren Sohn ...
I'm sorry to have to trouble you; it's about your son ...
Bei der Silvesterfahrt handelt es sich um eine Sieben-Tage-Tour.
The New Year's Eve trip is (a matter of) a seven-day tour.
Im Allgäu lebt es sich sehr angenehm.
Life is very pleasant in the Allgäu.

VOCABULARY

Here are some new words from this week and for the conversation that follows:

der	**Schmerz (-en)**	pain
	stark	strong
der	**Fehler (-)**	fault
	sich beschweren (I)	to complain
	erscheinen (I)	to appear
der	**Kassenbon (-s)**	sales receipt
der	**Kauf (⁻e)**	buying, purchase
die	**Reklamation (-en)**	complaint (here implying replacement or refund)
der	**Aufkleber (-)**	sticker
der	**Anfang (⁻e)**	beginning
	pfeifen	to whistle
der	**Pfeifton**	whistling
	auftauchen (II)	to turn up, to appear
der	**Ton (⁻e)**	sound
	sich (DO) anhören (II)	to sound
das	**Gerät (-e)**	(piece of) equipment
	überhaupt	at all, anyway
die	**Ordnung**	order
	einwandfrei	perfect
	genau	precisely, for certain
	versuchen (I)	to try
	allerdings	although, however
	ersetzen (I)	to refund
das	**Exemplar (-e)**	copy
	vorrätig	in stock
	bestellen (I)	to order
	sich (IO) anhören (II)	to listen to
	reichen	to hand
	sich vertun (I)	to make a mistake, to slip up

11

A customer returns a faulty CD to the shop

VERKÄUFER Ja, bitte schön?

KUNDIN Guten Tag! Ich habe mir vorgestern bei Ihnen eine CD mit Popmusik gekauft, die leider einige Defekte hat. Da die CD ziemlich teuer war, wollte ich mich jetzt beschweren.

VERKÄUFER Um was für eine CD handelt es sich denn?

KUNDIN Es ist das neueste Konzert von den Pur-Tops, das gerade erst erschienen ist.

VERKÄUFER Darf ich mal den Kassenbon sehen, den Sie beim Kauf bekommen haben, denn ohne Bon gibt es keine Reklamation.

KUNDIN Das Dumme ist, dass ich den Bon einfach nicht finden kann, aber Sie sehen, der Aufkleber mit dem Preis befindet sich noch auf der Hülle.

VERKÄUFER Ja, aber trotzdem ... Also, um welche Defekte handelt es sich denn?

KUNDIN Also, am Anfang gibt es einen hohen Pfeifton, der immer wieder auftaucht. Und dann hat die CD Stellen, wo man überhaupt nichts hört. Und wenn mal die Musik da ist, liegt das Ganze viel zu hoch im Ton.

VERKÄUFER Das hört sich nicht gut an, aber ist Ihr Gerät denn überhaupt in Ordnung?

KUNDIN O ja, das Gerät ist einwandfrei. Das weiß ich ganz genau, weil mein Bruder, der Musik studiert, seine CDs gespielt hat, nachdem ich es mit dieser versucht habe.

VERKÄUFER Na gut. Ich kann allerdings kein Geld ersetzen, sondern Ihnen nur ein neues Exemplar derselben CD geben, wenn wir sie noch vorrätig haben. Sonst muss ich sie bestellen ... Aber erst muss ich mir selbst die CD anhören.

11

KUNDIN	Bitte schön. [Sie reicht ihm die CD-Hülle und er macht sie auf.]
VERKÄUFER	Aber das ist doch kein Pur-Tops-Konzert, sondern das Klarinettenquintett von Mozart!
KUNDIN	O, da muss ich mich aber entschuldigen, ich habe mich vertan! Ich habe die Falsche mitgebracht!

TRANSLATION

ASSISTANT	Yes, can I help you?
CUSTOMER	Hello. The day before yesterday I bought a CD of pop music here (lit. "at yours"), which unfortunately is faulty. As the CD was rather expensive, I wanted to make a complaint.
ASSISTANT	What sort of CD is it?
CUSTOMER	It's the latest concert by the Pur-Tops, which has only just come out.
ASSISTANT	Can I see the sales receipt that you got at the time of purchase, since without a receipt there's no refund (lit. "claim").
CUSTOMER	The stupid thing is that I just can't find the receipt, but you can see that the sticker with the price on it is still on the case.
ASSISTANT	Yes, but still … So what were the faults?
CUSTOMER	Well, at the beginning there's a high-pitched whistling sound that keeps coming back. And then there are places on the CD where you can't hear anything at all. And when the music actually is there, everything is pitched much too high.
ASSISTANT	That doesn't sound good, but is your equipment working correctly?
CUSTOMER	Oh yes, the equipment is perfect. I know that for certain, because my brother, who's a music student, played his CDs after I tried to play this one ("with this one have tried").

11

ASSISTANT All right then. However, I can't refund cash but can only give you a new copy of the same CD, if we still have it in stock. Otherwise I'll have to order it ... But first I need to listen to the CD myself.

CUSTOMER Here you are. [She hands him the CD case and he opens it.]

ASSISTANT But this isn't a Pur-Tops concert, it's Mozart's Clarinet Quintet!

CUSTOMER Oh, I really must apologize. I've made a mistake! I've brought the wrong one!

Week 12

- *more on the formation and uses of the simple past*
- *the past perfect (e.g., "had walked")*
- *the formation and uses of the general subjunctive*
- *conditional statements in various time frames ("if he stays, we will ..."), ("if he stayed, we would ..."), ("if he had stayed, we would have ...")*
- *the passive with **zu** + infinitive*
- *idiomatic particles that express the attitude of the speaker*

12.1 MORE ON THE SIMPLE PAST TENSE

As we've seen, the simple past is an alternative to the present perfect for talking about something that occurred in the past: e.g., "I went," "I was going" (section 10.10). It is often called the narrative past because it is used to recount a series of connected events in the past. It is more common in formal writing—the present perfect is usually used conversationally.

Apart from the above, which tense you use depends on (a) if you want to reduce the number of words in a sentence (the simple past is a single-word tense); (b) if you want the main verb rather than an auxiliary verb in the second position; (c) if you want to create variety in complex sentences with more than one clause; (d) the rhythm of a sentence; and (e) regional speech habits.

Unlike in English, the choice is not determined by whether the action is fully completed (English past tense) or is continuing into the present (English present perfect). In German these tenses can be mixed in a sentence, with different tenses in different clauses:

simple past	present perfect
Als ich ankam,	**hat sie mich zu einer Tasse Kaffee eingeladen.**
When I arrived	she invited me for a cup of coffee.

12

There are two conjugation patterns: (a) one adds endings to the existing verb stem; (b) the other has a stem vowel change, plus adds endings in all persons except for the first- and third-person singular:

	same-stem verbs*	new-stem verbs**
ich	-(e)te	-
du	-(e)test	-(e)st
er/sie/es	-(e)te	-
wir	-(e)ten	-en
ihr	-(e)tet	-t
sie/Sie	-(e)ten	-en

* **e** is inserted when the stem ends in **-d** or **-t**
** **e** is inserted when the stem ends in **-s**, **-ss**, or **-ß**

Was du lasest, kam von der Kirche.
What you were reading came from the church.
Die Kinder machten ziemlich viel Krach, während er redete.
The children were making quite a lot of noise while he was speaking.

Once you've learned the conjugation endings, forming the simple past of same-stem verbs is straightforward, but the vowel change in new-stem verbs has to be learned (see section 12.2).

As well as (a) and (b) above, there are (c) a few new-stem verbs that take the same-stem verb endings:

infinitive		past tense stem
brennen	to burn	**brann-**
bringen	to bring, to take	**brach-**
denken	to think	**dach-**
kennen	to know (someone)	**kann-**
wissen	to know (a fact)	**wuss-**

Dass du ihn kanntest, wusste ich nicht.
I didn't know that you used to know him.

12

12.2 STEM-CHANGING VERBS IN THE PAST

Like all irregular verb forms, the stem change for new-stem verbs just has to be learned—there is no general rule for the way they change. Note that some of the new stems are the same as the stem of the past participle (see section 9.7), while others have unique changes.

Here are some commonly used verbs grouped according to whether or not the stem is the same as the past participle. (In these verbs, the simple-past stem is used for the first- and third-person singular with no endings.)

(1) Simple-past stem = past-participle stem

infinitive		past-tense stem (1st- & 3rd-person sing.)
stehen	to stand	**stand-**
leiden	to suffer	**litt-**
pfeifen	to whistle	**pfiff-**
schneiden	to cut	**schnitt-**
streiten	to quarrel	**stritt-**
bleiben	to stay, to remain	**blieb-**
leihen	to lend	**lieh-**
scheinen	to seem, to shine	**schien-**
schreiben	to write	**schrieb-**
steigen	to climb	**stieg-**
treiben	to drive, to impel	**trieb-**
riechen	to smell	**roch-**
schließen	to shut, to close	**schloss-**
bieten	to offer	**bot-**
fliegen	to fly	**flog-**
fliehen	to flee	**floh-**
ziehen	to pull, to draw	**zog-**
lügen	to lie (fib)	**log-**

(2) Simple-past stem ≠ past-participle stem: the latter is given for comparison. Note that if the main vowel in the

12

stem of the infinitive is **-e-** or **-i-** (but not both), the past-tense stem is almost certain to contain the vowel **-a-**. While this is not true of **wissen** (**wuss-**) or **gehen** (**ging-**), it works for all the other verbs in group (c) of section 12.1, for **stehen** in section (1), and for the following verbs:

infinitive		past-tense stem (1st- & 3rd-person sing.)	past participle
essen	to eat	**aß-**	**gegessen**
fahren	to go (not on foot)	**fuhr-**	**gefahren**
fangen	to catch	**fing-**	**gefangen**
geben	to give	**gab-**	**gegeben**
halten	to hold	**hielt-**	**gehalten**
kommen	to come	**kam-**	**gekommen**
laufen	to run, walk	**lief-**	**gelaufen**
lesen	to read	**las-**	**gelesen**
messen	to measure	**maß-**	**gemessen**
rufen	to call (out)	**rief-**	**gerufen**
schlafen	to sleep	**schlief-**	**geschlafen**
schlagen	to hit, beat	**schlug-**	**geschlagen**
sehen	to see	**sah-**	**gesehen**
stoßen	to bump, push	**stieß-**	**gestoßen**
tragen	to carry, wear	**trug-**	**getragen**
treten	to step, kick	**trat-**	**getreten**
wachsen	to grow	**wuchs-**	**gewachsen**
gehen	to go	**ging-**	**gegangen**
brechen	to break	**brach-**	**gebrochen**
helfen	to help	**half-**	**geholfen**
sprechen	to speak	**sprach-**	**gesprochen**
sterben	to die	**starb-**	**gestorben**
treffen	to meet	**traf-**	**getroffen**
nehmen	to take	**nahm-**	**genommen**
stehlen	to steal	**stahl-**	**gestohlen**
sitzen	to sit	**saß-**	**gesessen**

schwimmen	to swim	schwamm-	geschwommen
finden	to find	**fand-**	**gefunden**
singen	to sing	**sang-**	**gesungen**
sinken	to sink	**sank-**	**gesunken**
springen	to jump	**sprang-**	**gesprungen**
trinken	to drink	**trank-**	**getrunken**
bitten	to ask, request	**bat-**	**gebeten**
liegen	to lie (recline)	**lag-**	**gelegen**

Exercise 1

Rewrite the following pairs of sentences, turning the first in each pair into a clause introduced by **während** ("while") and using the second as the main clause. Use the simple past tense in the subordinate clause and the present perfect in the main clause. The first pair has been done for you.

1 Ich laufe durch die Stadt.
   Meine Schwester schläft.

   Während ich durch die Stadt lief, hat meine Schwester geschlafen.

2 Alex arbeitet im Garten.
   Sein Bruder hört sich Musik an.

3 Hanna schreibt einen Brief.
   Ihre Freundin geht schwimmen.

4 Markus trinkt Milch.
   Sein Bruder Anton trinkt Wasser.

5 Frau Krause spricht mit ihrem Nachbarn.
   Ein Einbrecher stiehlt ihr Geld vom Küchentisch.

6 Die Eltern streiten sich oben im Haus.
   Die Kinder halten unten im Haus eine Party.

7 Emil spricht mit den Eltern.
   Lea fängt den Hund ein.

12

12.3 THE PAST PERFECT (E.G., "I HAD BEEN")

This is formed with the simple past tense of **haben** or
sein + past participle. (For whether to use **sein** or **haben**
as the auxiliary, see section 9.5.) The past perfect is used
in the same way as in English (e.g., "I had walked/had
been walking") to make the sequence of events clear:

Als ich ankam, hatten sie (schon) gegessen.
When I arrived they had (already) eaten.
When I arrived they had (already) been eating.

as opposed to

Sobald ich ankam, aßen sie.
When (i.e., After) I arrived they ate.

or

Als ich ankam, aßen sie (schon/gerade).
When I arrived they were (already/just) eating.

It is also used to refer to situations or events preceding
a point or period of time that is already in the past:

**Bis vorgestern hatten wir keine Briefe von
ihm bekommen**.
Up to the day before yesterday, we hadn't received
any letters from him.

12.4 THE GENERAL SUBJUNCTIVE

The subjunctive mood is a verb form used to express
something unreal, possible, or hypothetical. While it exists
in English, its use isn't frequent. However, it is important
to learn in German.

There are two subjunctive moods in German. The most
frequently used is the general subjunctive (known in
German as subjunctive II). It is used in conditional
sentences, to express wishes, or to make polite requests.

12

We'll start by looking at the subjunctive conjugations of **haben** and the modal verbs, as these are forms that are in constant use.

The good news is that the general subjunctive forms are very similar—in some cases identical—to the simple past forms. Below you can see that the only difference is the addition of an umlaut for stems in **a**, **o**, or **u** (except for **sollen**). The endings **-e**, **-est**, **-e**, **-en**, **-et**, **-en** are added to the stem. The 1st-/3rd-person singular is given below.

past tense	general subjunctive	
hatte	**hätte**	would have, might have
war	**wäre**	would be, were (as in "if I were you …")
wurde	**würde**	would
durfte	**dürfte**	might; (negative) shouldn't
konnte	**könnte**	could, might, would be able to
mochte	**möchte**	would like (to)
musste	**müsste**	would have to
sollte	**sollte**	should, ought to, would be supposed to

Hättest du etwas dagegen?
Would you have any objection?
An deiner Stelle wäre ich böse.
In your place I would be angry.
Würden Sie bitte warten?
Would you please wait?
Er dürfte eigentlich nicht Auto fahren.
He shouldn't really be driving.
Er könnte sich verletzen.
He might hurt himself.
Ich möchte bitte eine Tasse Kaffee.
I'd like a cup of coffee, please.
Dieser Brief müsste übermorgen schon ankommen.
This letter needs to arrive the day after tomorrow.
Du solltest nicht so schnell fahren.
You shouldn't drive so fast.

12

12.5 MORE ON THE GENERAL SUBJUNCTIVE

As the forms of the general subjunctive are identical to the simple past tense for same-stem verbs (see section 12.1), to avoid confusion, a different construction with the subjunctive of **werden (würde, würdest, würde, würden, würdet, würden**, meaning "would") + infinitive is frequently used.

So although you might hear the following:
Wenn er ein neues Haus baute, ...

In everyday speech, the below is far more common:
Wenn er ein neues Haus bauen würde
If he built a new house, ...

The exceptions are **sein, haben,** and the modal verbs we saw in the previous section, so that's why the subjunctive forms of those verbs are important to learn.

In new-stem verbs, the subjunctive is distinguishable from the simple past in at least the first- and third-person singular, as these verbs use the stem of the simple past and add the endings **-e, -est, -e, -en, -et, -en**. And if the main vowel in the new stem is **a, o,** or **u**, all persons differ, as an umlaut is added in the subjunctive: **ä, ö,** or **ü**.

Here are the general subjunctive conjugations of some common new-stem verbs.

infinitive		**bleiben** (to stay)	**kommen** (to come)	**ziehen** (to pull)	**wissen** (to know)
past-tense new stem		**blieb-**	**kam-**	**zog-**	**wusste-**
general subjunctive					
ich	(¨)e	**bliebe**	**käme**	**zöge**	**wüsste**
du	(¨)est	**bliebest**	**kämest**	**zögest**	**wüsstest**
er/sie/es	(¨)e	**bliebe**	**käme**	**zöge**	**wüsste**
wir	(¨)en	**blieben**	**kämen**	**zögen**	**wüssten**
ihr	(¨)et	**bliebet**	**kämet**	**zöget**	**wüsstet**
sie/Sie	(¨)en	**blieben**	**kämen**	**zögen**	**wüssten**

12

12.6 CONDITIONAL STATEMENTS ("IF... THEN...")

As mentioned, one of the main uses of the general subjunctive is in conditional statements. A conditional statement consists of a subordinate clause expressing the condition and usually beginning with **wenn** (if), or less commonly **falls** (in case), and a main clause that expresses what will happen if the condition is met.

The verb form used in these statements depends on how likely it is the condition will be met. For instance, in the examples below, the present tense is used, as this is quite plausible. The order of the clauses can be reversed:

Wenn sie zu Hause bleibt, bringen wir ihr etwas Schönes mit.
If she stays at home we'll bring her something nice.
Wir bringen ihr etwas Schönes mit, wenn sie zu Hause bleibt.
We'll bring her something nice if she stays at home.

If the clause with the condition comes first:

(a) An alternative to using a linking word and placing the verb last (see section 11.4) is to start the clause with the verb, followed immediately by the subject:

Bleibt sie zu Hause, bringen wir ihr etwas Schönes mit.

It is important not to mistake this structure for a question.

(b) The main clause can start with **so** or **dann**:

Wenn sie zu Hause bleibt, so bringen wir ihr etwas Schönes mit.
Bleibt sie zu Hause, so bringen wir ihr etwas Schönes mit.
Wenn sie zu Hause bleibt, dann bringen wir ihr etwas Schönes mit.
Bleibt sie zu Hause, dann bringen wir ihr etwas Schönes mit.

12

There are three kinds of conditional statements in German, corresponding roughly to those in English.

(1) Odds are even on the condition being met, so neutral

In this context, the verb in the clause expressing the condition is conjugated in the present tense, and the verb in the main clause can be conjugated in the present or the future tense.

Wenn die Bäume schnell wachsen, bekommen wir in zwei Jahren die ersten Früchte.
If the trees grow fast, we'll get ("we get") the first fruit in two years. (present/present)
Wenn man ihm die Wahl eines Instruments überlässt, wird er bestimmt Klavier lernen.
If the choice of an instrument is left to him, he'll definitely learn the piano. (present/future)

(2) Odds are against the condition being met, so remote

Here the verbs of both clauses can be:

• either conjugated in the general subjunctive (section 12.5).

• or conjugated using the general subjunctive of **werden** (**ich/er/sie/es würde**, **du würdest**, **wir/sie/Sie würden**, **ihr würdet**) + infinitive.

Either option is fine. The main thing to remember is that unlike conditional sentences in English, the subjunctive must be used in both parts of the sentence.

Wenn wir so einen Mann in den Club aufnehmen würden, würden wir in Schwierigkeiten kommen.
or
Wenn wir so einen Mann in den Club aufnähmen, kämen wir in Schwierigkeiten.
If we accepted ("would accept") a man like that into the club, we would have difficulties. (subjunctive/subjunctive)

12

There is no need for consistency between the clauses—in fact variation is often preferred. However, as we've mentioned, **würde** + infinitive is very common in everyday speech. It has two advantages:

- many verbs (i.e., same-stem verbs) are identical in the simple past and subjunctive.

- if you're not sure of the subjunctive conjugation of a new-stem verb, you can get around this by using the **würde** construction. Of course, that makes it essential to learn the subjunctive forms of **werden**.

(3) The condition cannot be met because it relates to a possibility in the past, so hypothetical

For statements that describe a hypothetical action in the past, the past tense of the general subjunctive is required.

This is a perfect tense, so uses either **haben** or **sein** (depending on the verb) conjugated in the subjunctive as the auxiliary + past participle. (These forms for **haben** are **ich/er/sie/es hätte, du hättest, wir/sie/Sie hätten, ihr hättet**, and for **sein** are **ich/er/sie/es wäre, du wärest, wir/sie/Sie wären, ihr wäret**.) Both **hätte** and **wäre** convey the meaning "would have."

Again, the past subjunctive must be used in both parts of the sentence, in contrast to English tense sequence.

Wenn wir das gewusst hätten, wären wir nicht gekommen.
If we had known ("would have known") that, we wouldn't have come. (past subjunctive/past subjunctive)

12

Exercise 2

(a) Write out each conditional clause from the left-hand column, adding the correct main clause from the right-hand column.

(b) Write out the complete sentences a second time, deleting **wenn** and starting with the conjugated verb. The first sentence has been done for you.

1 (a) Wenn Emil in den Film geht, dann sehe ich ihn mir auch an.

1 (b) Geht Emil in den Film, dann sehe ich ihn mir auch an.

1 Wenn Emil in den Film geht, …	… dann wird es zu kalt für uns alle.
2 Wenn du die Fahrkarte besorgen würdest, …	… dann wäre sie schwierig.
3 Wenn Peter nicht das Fenster schließt, …	… dann wird es Krach geben.
4 Wenn dieser Mann nicht den Club verlässt, …	… dann sehe ich ihn mir auch an.
5 Wenn die kleine Tochter nicht fernsehen dürfte, …	… dann wirst du am Sonntagmorgen schlafen können
6 Wenn der Vater in die Kneipe (= pub) geht, …	… dann hätten wir die Möglichkeit, am Wochenende in die Berge zu fahren.
7 Wenn du jetzt das Essen für Sonntag kochst, …	… dann sitzt er immer draußen.

12

12.7 THE PASSIVE WITH **ZU** + INFINITIVE

We've seen how in a clause with **zu** + infinitive, this has to be in the final position (see section 10.5). In the **zu** clause, the implied subject of the verb is either the subject or the direct object in the main clause:

Wir haben vor, morgen in die Berge zu fahren.
We intend to drive into the mountains tomorrow.
(we intend … we drive)
Ich möchte dich bitten, mir die Fahrkarte zu besorgen.
I'd like to ask you to get the ticket for me.
(ask you … you get)
Wir helfen ihnen, den Weg zu finden.
We'll help them find the way.
(help them … they find)

However, **zu** + infinitive can also be used with **sein** to form the passive voice, in which case it is not a separate clause. It still appears at the end of the sentence:

Die Ergebnisse sind sofort nach der Wahl bekannt zu machen.
The results are to be made known immediately after the election.
(conveys a sense of obligation)
Dieser Wein ist in jedem Supermarkt zu bekommen.
This wine is available ("to obtain") at any supermarket.
(conveys a sense of possibility)
Dem Patienten ist nicht mehr zu helfen.
The patient cannot be helped ("is not more to be helped").
(conveys a sense of impossibility)
Sogar über den Direktor ist Kritik zu hören.
Criticism can even be heard about the director.
(conveys a sense of permission)

12

Note that the corresponding English construction of "to be" + "to" + infinitive does not necessarily form the passive but can express the future, or an obligation, or both. For example:

The meeting is to reconvene at 7:30.
(the meeting is going to/must reconvene)

12.8 IDIOMATIC PARTICLES THAT EXPRESS MOOD

In German there are a number of short words, usually unstressed, that have no direct translation in English, and which are not strictly necessary to the "factual" meaning of a sentence. They are known as modal particles or fillers, and they are used to reflect or reinforce mood or attitude.

Their role is not unlike the English idiomatic usage of words such as "(un)fortunately," "sadly," and "clearly," which are included to show how the speaker feels about what they are saying (and, often, how they hope to make the listener feel about it).

Our friends clearly can't finance the undertaking.

Here, "clearly" indicates that the speaker feels this is an obvious fact. This is different from the use of the same word below:

She stated her intentions clearly.

Here, "clearly" is a factual description of the verb.

The same is true of the two different uses of "hopefully" in the following:

Hopefully, he'll pass his driving test this time.
He embarked hopefully on his third attempt at a balloon crossing of the English Channel.

These expressions include words such as "probably" and "possibly," by which speakers give their assessment of how likely a statement is to be realized. Such expressions serve as a speaker's own comments on the content of what they are saying. German has similar expressions, such as **wahrscheinlich** (probably), **offensichtlich** (clearly), and **hoffentlich** (hopefully).

In addition, German also has a variety of little words that convey the attitude of the speaker. They have few counterparts in English, except "even."

Here are the most common of these modal particles, in order of frequency of use. As they are idiomatic, it's impossible to illustrate their use out of context, so we've just provided a rough description of the attitude each one expresses. Most of them are used in the conversation on p.196 (where we've underlined them).

doch	contradiction; objection; protest; persuasion
ja	acknowledgment by the speaker that the "fact" being stated is well known, accepted, obvious
wohl	belief that the "fact" being stated, though not definite, is highly probable; assumption
mal	minimalization of the "fact" stated (like "just" in English)
denn	impatience/urgency for an answer/explanation
etwa	vagueness; uncertainty; disbelief; incredulity
auch	mark or expectation of surprise at the inclusion of something in some notional category (like "even" in English)
schon	mark or expectation of surprise at the relative prematurity of something on some notional scale (like "even" in English)

12

noch	mark or expectation of surprise at the relative "overdueness" of something on some notional scale (like "even" in English)
eben (N. German) **halt** (S. German)	acceptance, acquiescence, resignation in the face of the inevitability of the "fact" being stated

These definitions are not literal and are only given as a guide.

Note, too, that all these words also have literal meanings: for example, **(je)doch** (however); **ja** (yes); **wohl** (well); **(ein)mal** (once); **denn** (for); **etwa** (about); **auch** (also); **schon** (already); **noch** (still); **eben** (just now).

VOCABULARY

die	**Kneipe (-n)**	bar
der	**Film (-e)**	film
der	**Fotoapparat (-e)**	camera
	nämlich	you see, in fact, as
	voll	full
die	**Sommerferien** (plural)	summer vacation
das	**Bild (-er)**	photo, picture
	vorig	last
das	**Taschengeld**	spending money
	sparen	to save
der	**Schulausflug (¨e)**	school trip
	Na gut.	All right then.
	verschieden	various
das	**Dia (-s)**	slide
	richtig	proper
der	**Augenblick (-e)**	moment
	im Augenblick	at present
	überreden (I)	to persuade
	hinterher	afterward
der	**Abzug (¨e)**	print
der	**Klassenkamerad (-en noun) / die Klassenkameradin (-nen)**	classmate
die	**Aufnahme (-n)**	exposure, photo
	Vierundzwanziger	with twenty-four
	reintun (II)	to put in
	so was	that sort of thing
	überhaupt	at all, in general
der	**Zähler (-)**	counter
	sich bewegen (I)	to move
	weiterdrehen (II)	to wind on
der	**Auslöser (-)**	shutter release
	drücken	to press
	egal ob	regardless of whether
	abgesehen davon	quite apart from that
	mach dir nichts daraus	don't worry about it
	kriegen	to get, to catch

12

What happens when a digital native tries out analog photography with her dad's film camera

TOCHTER Vati, sag <u>mal</u>, könntest du mir <u>wohl</u> bitte einen Film für deinen Fotoapparat geben? Die letzte Filmrolle ist nämlich voll. Ich habe ihn <u>schon</u> seit den Sommerferien darin und habe die letzten Bilder vorige Woche auf der Hochzeit von Marianne gemacht.

VATER Ich verstehe, du möchtest <u>wohl</u> dein Taschengeld sparen! Wenn ich dir einen Film gebe, brauchst du natürlich keinen zu kaufen.

TOCHTER Nein, so ist das nicht. Heutzutage ist so etwas schwer zu finden und wir haben heute einen Schulausflug, und ich möchte gern fotografieren können.

VATER Na gut. Ich habe verschiedene Filme. Was für einen wolltest du haben – für Dias oder richtige Bilder?

TOCHTER Im Augenblick ist da ein Diafilm drin. Du weißt, du hattest mich überredet, Dias zu machen. Aber ich habe richtige Bilder lieber, und die sind <u>auch</u> für einen Schulausflug besser. Ich könnte dann hinterher <u>auch</u> Abzüge für meine Klassenkameraden machen lassen.

VATER Gut. Wie viele Aufnahmen möchtest du <u>denn</u> haben? Möchtest du einen Vierundzwanziger-Film haben oder einen Sechsunddreißiger?

TOCHTER Gib mir <u>doch</u> einen Vierundzwanziger, dann ist der Film schneller zu Ende, denn für einen Schulausflug brauche ich <u>doch</u> bloß zehn oder so.

VATER [Er reicht ihr einen Film.] So, da hast du deinen Film ...

12

TOCHTER ... und Vati, könntest du <u>mal</u> bitte den alten Film herausnehmen und den neuen reintun? Du weißt ja, ich kenne diesen Fotoapparat noch nicht so gut ...

VATER Na gut ... [Er öffnet den Fotoapparat.] Aber hier ist <u>doch</u> überhaupt kein alter Film drin! Hast du <u>etwa</u> die ganze Zeit ohne Film fotografiert?!

TOCHTER Was??!! Meine schönen Aufnahmen von der Hochzeit und überhaupt aus den ganzen Wochen seit den Sommerferien! Und ich dachte die ganze Zeit, es wäre ein Film drin! Der Zähler bewegte sich <u>doch</u> immer weiter.

VATER Bei diesem Apparat geht der Zähler <u>eben</u> weiter, wenn man weiterdreht und den Auslöser drückt, egal ob ein Film drin ist oder nicht. Abgesehen davon wüsste ich nicht, wie ein Film überhaupt in diesem Apparat hätte sein können. Ich habe nämlich den alten Film am Ende der Ferien selbst herausgenommen. Aber mach dir nichts daraus! Du kriegst Abzüge von meinen Hochzeitsbildern!

TRANSLATION

DAUGHTER Dad, (tell me,) could you give me film for your camera, please? (You see,) the last roll is finished (lit. "full"). I've had it in since the summer vacation, and I took the last photos last week at Marianne's wedding.

FATHER I see, you'd like to save your spending money! If I give you film, you won't need to buy one, of course.

DAUGHTER No, it's not (like) that. These days it's hard to find, and we have a school trip today, and I'd like to be able to take some photographs.

12

FATHER	All right. I have various types of film. What sort did you want (to have): for slides or photos?
DAUGHTER	At the moment it has slide film. (You) remember, you'd persuaded me to take slides. But I prefer photos, and they're better for a school trip. Then I'd be able to get prints made for my classmates afterward.
FATHER	Fine. How many exposures would you like (to have)? Do you want a twenty-four exposure film or one with thirty-six?
DAUGHTER	Let me have one with twenty-four. (Then) the film will be finished more quickly, (since) I only need about ten for a school trip.
FATHER	[He hands her film.] Well, there's your film …
DAUGHTER	… and Dad, could you please just take the old film out and put the new one in? You know I don't know this camera very well yet …
FATHER	Oh, all right … [He opens the camera.] But there isn't any old film (at all) in here! Surely you haven't been taking photographs all this time without film in it?!
DAUGHTER	What??!! My lovely photos of the wedding, and from all these weeks since (the start of) the summer vacation! And all the time I thought there was film in it! But the counter kept going.
FATHER	In this camera the counter does advance when you wind on and press the shutter release, regardless of whether there's film in it or not. But, apart from that, I can't see how film could have been in the camera. (You see,) I took the old film out myself at the end of the vacation. But don't worry about it! You'll get prints of my photographs of the wedding!

Week 13

- *the present participle (the -ing form) and different ways this is expressed in German*
- *linking words such as "therefore," "however," etc.*
- *addressing a group informally (ihr: "you" plural)*
- *word order in sentences with two infinitives*
- *idiomatic use of impersonal expressions*
- *uses and formation of the special subjunctive*
- *the subjunctive in reported speech*
- *participle clauses*

13.1 THE PRESENT PARTICIPLE (THE -ING FORM) AND ALTERNATIVES TO USING IT

The present participle (the -ing form in English) is normally formed by adding **-d** to the infinitive:
reisen to travel **reisend** traveling

In German, the most common use of the present participle is as an adjective in front of the noun (see section 11.2):

der lachende Polizist
the laughing policeman

We'll find out more about this usage in section 13.9.

Apart from this, there are few direct German equivalents for the various uses of the present participle in English. In examples such as the following, German would use an alternative verb form:

After talking to him I changed my mind.
After I talked to him I changed my mind.
Nachdem ich mit ihm gesprochen hatte, habe ich meine Meinung geändert.

Before leaving I gave them my phone number.
Before I left I gave them my phone number.
Bevor ich wegging, habe ich ihnen meine Telefonnummer gegeben.

13

However, for expressions such as "by ...-ing" and "in spite of ...-ing," there are no corresponding equivalents in German, which requires constructions such as those in section 11.4 (3b).

(1) Expressing "by ...-ing"

Use **indem** to introduce a subordinate clause:

Ich konnte viel Geld sparen, indem ich Überstunden gemacht habe.
I was able to save a lot of money by working overtime ("in that I did overtime").

(2) Expressing "in spite of ...-ing"

Use **trotzdem** to introduce a subordinate clause:

Ich konnte nicht viel Geld sparen, trotzdem ich Überstunden gemacht habe.
I wasn't able to save much money in spite of working overtime ("in spite of that I did overtime").

These constructions allow the main and subordinate clause to have different subjects:

Wir konnten viel Geld sparen, indem du Überstunden gemacht hast.
We were able to save a lot of money by your working overtime.

13

13.2 MORE LINKING WORDS

The last conversation contained two examples of
nämlich (namely, actually, in fact, that is to say):

Meiner ist nämlich voll.

**Ich habe nämlich den alten Film . . . selbst
herausgenommen.**

The term **nämlich** indicates that the sentence containing
it is an explanation of something previously stated.

Whereas the conjunctions we saw in section 11.4 enable
clauses or sentences to be joined together, there are a
number of linking words that can be used more flexibly,
for example, within a phrase, and point to the way a train
of thought is developing.

Some of the most common of these terms follow,
grouped by function and with the nearest English
equivalents. They are given without examples, because
they can only be properly illustrated in the context of
longer sequences. You will find many examples in the
conversation at the end of this week.

Most of these terms can stand at the start or in
the middle of a sentence, but any restrictions on their
position are noted.

(1) Consequential

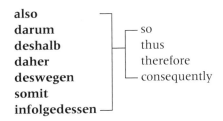

also
darum   so
deshalb   thus
daher   therefore
deswegen   consequently
somit
infolgedessen

NOTE: German **also** never means "also," and **so** on its own usually means "in this way" (although before an adjective it means "so").

(2) Explanatory

denn (start only)
nämlich (middle only)

for, because, in that case
in fact, actually, you see

(3) Additive

außerdem
überdies
zudem

besides, furthermore,
  moreover

ebenfalls
gleichfalls

likewise

(4) Dismissive

ohnehin (middle only)
sowieso (middle only)

anyway, in any case

(5) Remonstrative

immerhin
schließlich

after all

wenigstens
jedenfalls

at least
at any rate

(6) Reservational

jedoch
doch (start only)

however

13

(7) Contrastive

andererseits	on the other hand,
dagegen	in contrast, by
hingegen	comparison

(8) Concessive

allerdings	admittedly, to be sure,
freilich	though (final only),
	mind you
zwar ... aber	true ... but

NOTE: **zwar** in this sense is always followed by **aber**, **jedoch**, or some similar reservational term in a subsequent sentence.

(9) Provocative

trotzdem	nevertheless,
dennoch	nonetheless

(10) Alternative

sonst	otherwise
ansonsten	
es sei denn	unless, except that

NOTE: **es sei denn** is very close in sense to the linking word **wenn** (if) followed by a negative (**nicht** or **kein**).

13

Exercise 1

Add an appropriate linking word from the list below to the second sentence of each pair. In some sentences more than one choice is possible, in which case the key gives the most apt word, with the others in parentheses. Try putting the terms at the start and in the middle of the sentence, making any other necessary changes. The first example has been done for you.

allerdings
andererseits
außerdem
deshalb
immerhin
jedoch
trotzdem

1 Emil weiß, dass Karl kommt.
Er plant eine Busfahrt mit ihm.

Deshalb plant er eine Busfahrt mit ihm.
Er plant deshalb eine Busfahrt mit ihm.

2 Karl möchte zur Nordsee.
Emil bucht eine Fahrt nach Berlin.

3 Berlin ist eine schöne Stadt.
Es gibt sehr viele Touristen.

4 Die Nordsee ist ruhig.
In Berlin gibt es viel zu sehen.

5 Das Brandenburger Tor ist sehr attraktiv.
Es ist historisch und politisch wichtig.

6 Warum ist es historisch und politisch wichtig?
Vor einiger Zeit war es das Tor zwischen Westen und Osten.

7 Karl wollte an die Nordsee.
Er hat Berlin sehr interessant gefunden.

13.3 ADDRESSING A GROUP INFORMALLY: THE PLURAL "YOU" (IHR)

We've seen how **du** is used to address one person informally (section 7.5), and **Sie** is used to address anyone (one or more than one person) formally.

Don't forget that there is also a third form, **ihr**, which is used for talking to more than one person you know well or are on casual terms with. This can be tricky for English speakers to get used to, so here is a reminder of the forms for the informal plural "you":

personal pronoun			possessive adjective	
SU	**ihr**	you	SU **euer** / **eure** your	
DO	**euch**	you	(m./n.) / (f./pl.)	
IO	**euch**	you	(see section 7.2 for the other declensions)	

ihr conjugations

	present tense	simple past	general subjunctive	imperative (commands)
haben	habt	hattet	hättet	habt
sein	seid	wart	wäret	seid
dürfen	dürft	durftet	dürftet	–
sollen	sollt	solltet	solltet	–
lassen	lasst	ließt	ließet	lasst
sehen	seht	saht	sähet	seht
machen	macht	machtet	machtet	macht
reden	redet	redetet	redetet	redet

13

13.4 SUBORDINATE CLAUSES WITH TWO INFINITIVES

A subordinate clause in which the conjugated verb comes last (see section 11.4) will contain two infinitives if a perfect tense of certain auxiliary verbs is used. Look at two examples from section 10.9:

Ich habe den Nachbarn helfen müssen.
Ich habe meinen Wagen waschen lassen.

If we turn them into subordinate clauses, in which the conjugated verb (here, **habe**) would normally stand last, it now comes immediately before the two infinitives:

Ich kam zu spät, weil ich den Nachbarn habe helfen müssen.
I came late because I had to help the neighbors.
Obwohl ich meinen Wagen habe waschen lassen, sah er hinterher immer noch schmutzig aus.
Although I had my car washed, it still looked dirty afterward.

13.5 IMPERSONAL EXPRESSIONS

Some German expressions use the third-person singular pronoun **es** as a "general" subject that doesn't specify a particular person or thing.

Certain of these are similar to English (e.g., **es regnet** it's raining), but some are more idiomatic. You already know **es gibt** (there is/are, section 6.2) and **es handelt sich (um)** (it concerns, section 11.6). Here are some more examples:

Bei Nacht ging es über die Grenze.
I [or whoever the context indicates] crossed the frontier by night.
Während der Revolution kam es zu gefährlichen Unruhen.
During the revolution some dangerous disturbances occurred.

Bei unseren Exportplänen geht es nur um den Kurs.
Regarding our export plans, it's solely a matter of the rate of exchange.

In these examples, **es** is obligatory, but it's optional in other idioms and is commonly left out in everyday speech.

Es ist mir zu warm, mach bitte das Fenster auf!
or
Mir ist zu warm, mach bitte das Fenster auf!
I'm too hot. Please open the window!

Es graut mir vor dem Schulanfang nach den Ferien.
or
Mir graut vor dem Schulanfang nach den Ferien.
I hate (the thought of) the start of school after the holidays.

13.6 THE SPECIAL SUBJUNCTIVE

This is the second form of the German subjunctive (known in German as subjunctive I), which was traditionally used to report the speech of a third person (see section 13.7). Today, it is rare in everyday speech and is almost exclusively used in the third-person singular. This is formed by adding **-e** to the stem of the infinitive. (The sole exception is **sein**, see below.) The only plural form much used is **seien** (from **sein**).

infinitive	3rd-person singular special subjunctive
haben	**habe**
sein	**sei**
dürfen	**dürfe**
sollen	**solle**
lassen	**lasse**
sehen	**sehe**
machen	**mache**
reden	**rede**
tun	**tue**

13

As in English, directly quoted speech in German is placed within quotation marks (although the style of quotation marks is a bit different, as you'll see in the examples).

In reported speech, German as in English always uses the third person: for instance, if the speaker says "I ...," this becomes "he" or "she" in reported speech, or "here" may become "there," etc.

However, a key difference in German is that in formal writing, such as newspapers or in broadcasts on the radio or TV (although rarely in everyday conversation), the subjunctive is used throughout for reporting speech. Here are some guidelines:

(1) Every present tense verb in the speaker's actual words (including the present tenses of **haben** and **sein** used as part of the present perfect or of **werden** as part of the future or the passive) is replaced by EITHER the special subjunctive OR the general subjunctive.

The main thing is that the verb should demonstrably be in the subjunctive. The special subjunctive should be used if its form is different from the present tense. However, with many verbs, the special subjunctive conjugation is the same as the present tense, so in that situation, the general subjunctive should be used.

However, very often the third-person singular (he/she) is used in reported speech, and this is always different from the present tense because the third-person singular in the special subjunctive ends in **-e** instead of **-t**. So, you would read or hear, for example:

Actual words	**Der Minister: „Ich nehme die ganze Verantwortung auf mich, denn der Fehler wird schwere Folgen haben."**
Reported speech	**Der Minister sagte, er nehme die ganze Verantwortung auf sich,**

13

denn der Fehler werde schwere Folgen haben.
The minister said he was taking the whole responsibility upon himself, for the error would have grave consequences.

Actual words	**Monika: „Ich nehme keinen Regenschirm mit, sonst lasse ich ihn bestimmt irgendwo liegen."**
Reported speech	**Monika sagte, sie nehme/nähme keinen Regenschirm mit, sonst lasse/ließe sie ihn bestimmt irgendwo liegen.** Monika said she wasn't taking an umbrella. Otherwise she would be certain to leave it somewhere.
Actual words	**Die Freunde: „Wir sind heute zu euch gekommen, weil wir euch seit langem nicht gesehen haben."**
Reported speech	**Unsere Freunde sagten, sie seien/wären heute zu uns gekommen, weil sie uns seit langem nicht gesehen hätten.** Our friends said they had come to (see) us today because they hadn't seen us for a long time.

NOTE:

(a) The general subjunctive is preferred in conversation.

(b) Just as **würde (-st, -n, -t)** + infinitive of the main verb is used in conditional statements (see section 12.6), it is also a useful substitute in reported speech, especially when no clear subjunctive form is available:

Actual words	**Die Nachbarn: „Wir erwarten unsere Tochter mit Mann und Kindern aus Würzburg für die Weihnachtsferien."**

13

Reported speech	**Unsere Nachbarn sagten, sie würden ihre Tochter mit Mann und Kindern aus Würzburg für die Weihnachtsferien erwarten.**
	Our neighbors said they were expecting their daughter with her husband and children from Würzburg for the Christmas holidays.

(2) Every past-tense verb in the speaker's actual words is replaced by the past subjunctive of that verb, which is formed with either the special or general subjunctive of **haben** or **sein** + past participle. The rule for the choice of the auxiliary is the same as for other perfect tenses:

Actual words	**Peter: „Ich fand nur drei Kunden vor, als ich das Geschäft aufmachte."**
Reported speech	**Peter sagt, er** $\left\{\begin{array}{l}\textbf{habe}\\\textbf{hätte}\end{array}\right\}$ **nur drei Kunden vorgefunden, als er das Geschäft aufgemacht** $\left\{\begin{array}{l}\textbf{habe}\\\textbf{hätte.}\end{array}\right.$
	Peter said he found only three customers (waiting) when he opened the shop.

Actual words	**Die Zwillinge: „Wir gingen zusammen bis zum Markt, wo wir uns dann trennten."**
Reported speech	**Die Zwillinge sagten, sie** $\left\{\begin{array}{l}\textbf{seien}\\\textbf{wären}\end{array}\right\}$ **zusammen bis zum Markt gegangen, wo sie sich dann getrennt hätten."**
	The twins said they went together as far as the market, where they then separated.

If the speaker's actual words are in the past perfect (see section 12.3), the **haben** or **sein** auxiliary is simply replaced with the subjunctive equivalent:

Actual words	**Die Gäste: „Wir waren zum Strand gegangen und als wir uns zum Sonnen**

13

	hingelegt hatten, fing es plötzlich an zu regnen.„
Reported speech	**Die Gäste sagten, sie wären zum Strand gegangen, und als sie sich zum Sonnen hingelegt hätten,** $\left\{\begin{matrix}\text{hätte}\\\text{habe}\end{matrix}\right\}$ **es plötzlich angefangen zu regnen.**
	The guests said they had gone to the beach and when they had lain down to sunbathe it suddenly started raining.

(3) When a speaker's actual words contain an imperative form of the verb (the command form), there is no hard and fast rule about how to report this indirectly. The natural way is to use either the general subjunctive **möchte** or some form of the verb **sollen**, subjunctive or not, as seems to fit the case:

Actual words	**Arzt: „Essen Sie nur Fisch oder mageres Fleisch!"**
Reported speech	**Der Arzt sagt, ich soll nur Fisch oder mageres Fleisch essen.**
	The doctor says I must only eat fish or lean meat.
Actual words	**Schwester und Schwager: „Geh zum Arzt!"**
Reported speech	**Die haben gemeint, ich soll zum Arzt gehen.**
	They said I must go to the doctor.
Actual words	**Arzthelferin: „Herr Doktor, schauen Sie bitte doch noch einmal bei Herrn Sinke vorbei."**
Reported speech	**Meine Helferin hat gesagt, ich sollte bei Ihnen noch einmal vorbeischauen.**
	My assistant told me to visit you again.
Actual words	**Hempels: „Bitte besuchen Sie uns doch, sobald wir das Haus eingerichtet haben!"**

13

Reported speech	**Hempels haben gesagt, wir möchten sie besuchen, sobald sie das Haus eingerichtet hätten.**
	The Hempels said we must visit them as soon as they had furnished the house.

13.8 WORD ORDER IN REPORTED SPEECH

Most of the examples in the previous section required no change in word order in reported speech. This is because no linking words were used to introduce the reported speech clauses. This is only possible with statements and instructions. Even these are often introduced by **dass**, and all reported questions must start with one of the linking words from section 11.4 (2). In these situations, the conjugated verb in the clause must stand at the end:

Actual words	**Mann: „Ich halte gar nichts von den Freunden unserer Kinder."**
Reported speech	**Mein Mann sagt, dass er gar nichts von den Freunden unserer Kinder halte/hielte.**
	My husband says that he doesn't think much of our children's friends.

Actual words	**Er: „Wie lange wirst du noch einkaufen?"**
Reported speech	**Er fragte sie, wie lange sie noch einkaufen** $\begin{cases} \textbf{werde} \\ \textbf{würde.} \end{cases}$
	He asked her how long she would go on shopping.

Actual words	**Ich: „Geben Sie meinem Sohn noch eine Chance?"**
Reported speech	**Ich fragte ihn, ob er meinem Sohn noch eine Chance** $\begin{cases} \textbf{gebe} \\ \textbf{gäbe.} \end{cases}$
	I asked him whether he would give my son another chance.

13

Exercise 2

For each example of reported speech, select which of the statements (a), (b), or (c) comes closest to the situation described.

1 Der Minister sagt, er habe den Brief vor drei Wochen zwar gesehen, aber er sei nicht überzeugt gewesen.

(a) Es gibt einen Brief.
(b) Es gibt keinen Brief.
(c) Ein Brief ist angekommen.

2 Monika sagt, sie habe ihren Regenschirm zuerst an der Schule liegen gelassen, ihn dann aber später abgeholt.

(a) Sie hat ihren Regenschirm verloren.
(b) Sie bringt ihren Regenschirm zur Schule.
(c) Sie hat ihren Regenschirm noch.

3 Die Freunde sagen, sie hätten uns lange nicht gesehen und würden uns gern besuchen.

(a) Die Freunde besuchen uns.
(b) Die Freunde möchten uns besuchen.
(c) Die Freunde möchten uns nicht sehen.

4 Die Nachbarn sagen, ihre Tochter spiele im Orchester Klarinette und ginge bald auf eine Reise nach England.

(a) Die Tochter geht auf Ferien nach England.
(b) Die Tochter spielt Klarinette in England.
(c) Die Nachbarn fahren nach England.

5 Peter sagt, er habe nur zwei Kunden am Morgen gehabt; am Nachmittag seien noch vier schwierige Kunden gekommen und er sei deshalb am Abend sehr müde gewesen.

(a) Peter hat sechs nette Kunden gehabt.
(b) Peter ist froh, dass es Abend ist.
(c) Peter bedient seine Kunden freundlich.

6 Die Zwillinge sagen, sie seien auf den Markt gegangen und hätten sich Pullover gekauft; einer von ihnen habe noch ein T-Shirt gekauft.

(a) Die Zwillinge haben zwei Pullover und zwei T-Shirts gekauft.
(b) Die Zwillinge haben sich auf dem Markt getrennt.
(c) Einer der Zwillinge hat einen Pullover und ein T-Shirt.

13

> **7** Die Gäste sagen, sie hätten sich erst am Strand
> sonnen wollen; sie hätten dann einen Ausflug
> machen wollen, aber die Sonne sei für alles zu
> heiß gewesen.
> (a) Die Gäste haben einen Ausflug gemacht.
> (b) Die Gäste haben sich gesonnt.
> (c) Die Gäste konnten das alles nicht machen.

13.9 PARTICIPLE CLAUSES

Section 11.4 (1) on relative pronouns (**der, die, das**, etc.)
showed how they link the clause they introduce to a noun
mentioned in a preceding clause. But sometimes a clause
can be placed before the noun to which it relates rather
than after it.

A clause before the noun must have that noun as its
subject, and the verb in the clause becomes a participle.
To illustrate this, let's take an example from section 11.4
where the relative pronoun is in the nominative case:

**Das Fleisch, das auf dem Tisch liegt, kannst du für
den Hund nehmen.** ("The meat, that lies on the table,
you can take for the dog.")

The clause could also appear as follows:
**Das [auf dem Tisch liegende] Fleisch kannst du für
den Hund nehmen.** ("The [on the table lying] meat you
can take for the dog.")

Three things have happened to this clause:

(a) the relative pronoun **das** has been dropped

(b) the conjugated verb **liegt** has changed into the present
participle **liegend** (lying) (see sections 11.2 and 13.1)

(c) **liegend** has acquired the ending needed by adjectives
after definite articles (see section 7.3), since although

liegend is not an adjective, it has to be treated like one in the same way as **das frische Fleisch** → **das auf dem Tisch liegende Fleisch.**

Apart from that, the word order is the same as in the original relative clause, with **liegend** occupying the position of the verb **liegt**. The participle clause would be the same if the time frame changed:

Das Fleisch, das auf dem Tisch lag, konntest du für den Hund nehmen.
Das [auf dem Tisch liegende] Fleisch konntest du für den Hund nehmen.
You were able to take the meat that was on the table for the dog.

There are restrictions on which type of word may appear last in participle clauses (note that these are almost always inserted between an article and the noun they relate to and include a participle).

There are five possible types of final word, depending on the characteristics of the original relative clause (in the following examples, the relative clause from which the participle clause is derived is given first). The final word in the clause can be:

(1) An adjective

Der Verlust der Reisepässe war eine Angelegenheit, die dem Reiseleiter äußerst unangenehm war.
The loss of the passports was a matter that was extremely embarrassing to the courier.
Der Verlust der Reisepässe war eine [dem Reiseleiter äußerst unangenehme] Angelegenheit.

Here the verb **war** from the original relative clause has disappeared in the participle clause.

(2) The present participle of almost any verb except **sein** and the auxiliary verbs (when they function as auxiliaries)

Teilnehmer, die bis morgen auf ihre Ergebnisse hier warten, werden eingeladen, im Hotel zu übernachten.

Participants who are waiting here until tomorrow for their results are invited to spend the night in the hotel.

[Bis morgen auf ihre Ergebnisse hier wartende] Teilnehmer werden eingeladen, im Hotel zu übernachten.

In this participle clause, there is no definite article, as this is also omitted in the original sentence. The conjugated verb **warten** becomes a present participle.

(3) The past participle of any verb that can have a DO

Das östliche Mittelmeer, das oft von meinen Bekannten als Lieblingsreiseziel ausgesucht wird, werde auch ich mir dieses Jahr vornehmen.

This year I'm also going to visit the eastern Mediterranean, which is often chosen by those I know ("my acquaintances") as a favorite destination.

Das [oft von meinen Bekannten als Lieblingsreiseziel ausgesuchte] östliche Mittelmeer werde auch ich mir dieses Jahr vornehmen.

Zündkerzen, die zu selten ausgewechselt wurden, können einen dann im Stich lassen.

Spark plugs that have been changed too infrequently can (then) leave you in the lurch.

[Zu selten ausgewechselte] Zündkerzen können einen dann im Stich lassen.

Here, the participle clauses omit the conjugated auxiliary verb **werden**. The past participles **ausgesucht** and **ausgewechselt** take an ending like an adjective. The second example does not start with a definite article.

(4) The past participle of a verb requiring **sein** in the perfect tenses

13

Die Stadt wird von einer Krankheit bedroht, die in der Gegend noch nie vorgekommen ist.
The town is threatened by a disease that has never before appeared in the area.
Die Stadt wird von einer [in der Gegend noch nie vorgekommenen] Krankheit bedroht.

This type of participle clause loses the conjugated auxiliary verb **sein** from the original clause. The past participle takes an ending like an adjective.

(5) zu + present participle of any verb that can take a DO

It might be helpful to refer back to section 12.7, from which the following examples derive:

Die Ergebnisse, die sofort nach der Wahl bekannt zu machen sind, werden im Rathaus ausgehängt.
The results, which are to be made known immediately after the election, will be posted in the town hall.
Die [sofort nach der Wahl bekannt zu machenden] Ergebnisse werden im Rathaus ausgehängt.

Die Kritik, die über den Direktor zu hören war, war unberechtigt.
The criticism that was to be heard about the director was unfounded.
Die [über den Direktor zu hörende] Kritik war unberechtigt.

Here, the conjugated form of **sein** disappears in the participle clause.

With all these examples, it is essential first to isolate the participle clause, then to establish which type of relative clause it is similar to. Finally, you need to understand it along the same lines as our translations of the original clauses. Participle clauses are found in profusion in German, especially in writing, so it's important to be able to recognize and understand them.

13

VOCABULARY

Here are some new words used in the conversation that follows:

	vorhaben (II)	to have planned
	genau	precisely
	hier ist nichts los	nothing's going on here
	um ... herum	about
	erzählen	to tell
	zustehen (II)	to be due
	vorschießen (II)	to advance (money)
	meines Erachtens	in my opinion
	wahnsinnig	crazy
	umgehen (mit) (II)	to deal (with)
die	**Verhältnisse** (plural)	conditions, circumstances
	ausgeben (II)	to spend
	grillen	to grill
	geeignet	suitable
	je	each
	besorgen (I)	to obtain
	so (et)was	things like that
die	**Tiefkühltruhe (-n)**	freezer (chest)
	toll	great, fantastic
	sich verschulden (I)	to get into debt, to go into the red
	überübermorgen	the day after the day after tomorrow
	übernachten (I)	to stay the night
	aufkommen (II)	to (be liable to) pay
	was = etwas	something
	übrigens	by the way
der	**Eintritt**	admission
	dabei wegkommen (mit) (II)	to get away (with)
	nicht in Frage kommen	to be out of the question
der	**Vorschuss (ˉe)**	advance
	gewiss	certainly

	anspruchslos	undemanding
die	Unterhaltung (-en)	entertainment
	in die Tasche greifen	to dip into one's pocket
	losfahren (II)	to set out, to come out
	abholen (II)	to collect, to pick up
die	Erziehung	education, upbringing
die	Sparsamkeit	thrift

CONVERSATION

A family controversy over teenagers' spending

VATER Was habt ihr denn heute Abend vor?

SOHN Das wissen wir noch nicht ganz genau. Hier in Vossdorf ist heute nichts los, aber in Wunsdorf soll es eine große Party mit bekannten DJs geben. Die wäre allerdings ziemlich teuer, so um die fünfundzwanzig Euro herum pro Person, hat uns die Brigitte erzählt ...

MUTTER ... und deswegen wollt ihr also nicht hin ...

TOCHTER ... O doch, wenn ihr uns das uns für die nächsten vier Wochen zustehende Taschengeld vorschießen würdet.

VATER Ihr habt eine meines Erachtens wahnsinnige Art, mit Geld umzugehen. Ihr lebt total über eure Verhältnisse. So viel braucht ihr doch wohl nicht für einen einzigen Abend auszugeben!

MUTTER Ja, Vater hat ganz Recht!

SOHN Es geht leider nicht nur um heute Abend! Morgen gibt's nämlich ein Barbecue bei Eckels, und der Leo hat gesagt, wir

13

möchten doch etwas zum Grillen und ein paar Getränke mitbringen.

MUTTER So was braucht ihr doch nicht zu kaufen! Ich werde für euch ein paar Sachen aus der Tiefkühltruhe holen, und Getränke könnt ihr auch von hier mitnehmen.

TOCHTER Oh, das wäre toll! Ich glaube, wir müssen uns trotzdem verschulden, denn überübermorgen gibt die Brigitte eine tolle Party bei ihr, und da wir auch dort übernachten dürfen, müssen wir ihrer Mutter natürlich ein Geschenk mitbringen.

MUTTER Wenn es sich um ein Geschenk für die Mutter handelt, braucht ihr doch nicht dafür aufzukommen! Ich besorge morgen was Schönes in der Stadt.

VATER Was möchtest du denn sonst noch finanzieren, Ilse?

SOHN Übrigens brauchen wir für heute Abend nicht nur den Eintritt sondern auch das Geld für ein Taxi hinterher von Wunsdorf bis nach Hause. Das sind immerhin fünfzehn Kilometer, und mit weniger als dreißig Euro Fahrtkosten kommen wir nicht dabei weg.

VATER Das macht zusammen etwa achtzig Euro für einen einzigen Abend! Das kommt überhaupt nicht in Frage, mit oder ohne Vorschuss!

MUTTER Was Vater sagt, ist ganz gewiss richtig, ihr müsstet viel anspruchsloser sein. Andererseits, für eine harmlose Unterhaltung mit Freunden einmal in der Woche braucht ihr nicht in eure eigene Tasche zu greifen. Den Eintritt können wir bezahlen. Außerdem sagt Vater immer, er führe nachts ganz gern los, um euch von irgendwo abzuholen. Also könnt ihr auch das Taxigeld sparen!

VATER Und das soll nun Erziehung zu Sparsamkeit sein!

13

FATHER   So what are you doing this evening?

SON   We don't exactly know yet. There's nothing going on here in Vossdorf, but there's supposed to be a big party with famous DJs in Wunsdorf. It's pretty expensive though, about 25 euros per person, that's what Brigitte told us …

MOTHER   … and so you're not intending to go then …

DAUGHTER   Oh we are, if you'd advance us the spending money that's due to us for the next four weeks.

FATHER   You have a way of dealing with money that's crazy in my opinion. You're living completely beyond your means. You're not telling me that you need to spend that much on a single evening!

MOTHER   Yes, your father's absolutely right!

SON   Unfortunately, it's not just a question of tonight. In fact, tomorrow there's a barbecue at the Eckels, and Leo said we should bring something to barbecue and a few drinks.

MOTHER   But you don't need to buy anything like that! I'll take a few things out of the freezer for you, and you can take some drinks from here, too.

DAUGHTER   Oh, that would be great! I still think we'll have to go into the red though. The day after the day after tomorrow Brigitte's giving a fantastic party at her house, and as we're allowed to stay the night there we've obviously got to take her mother a present.

MOTHER   If it's a present for her mother, you don't have to spend your money on it! I'll get something nice in town tomorrow.

FATHER   And what else were you thinking of underwriting, Ilse?

SON   By the way, for this evening we don't only need the admission, but also the money for a taxi home from Wunsdorf afterward. After all, that's fifteen kilometers, and we won't get away with a fare less than 30 euros.

13

FATHER Altogether that's about 80 euros for a single evening! That's quite out of the question, with or without an advance!

MOTHER What your father says is quite right. You ought to be a lot less demanding. On the other hand, you don't need to dip into your own pockets for a bit of harmless entertainment with friends once a week. We can pay the admission charge. Moreover, your dad's always saying how he's happy to come out at night to pick you up from somewhere or other. So you'll even be able to save the taxi fare!

FATHER And that's what you call bringing them up to be careful with money!

13

Reading practice

Eine Reise durch Europa

Als ich eine Einladung zu einer Hochzeit in Verona, Italien, erhielt, war ich total aufgeregt. Ich könnte den Zug nehmen und eine Tour durch Europa machen! Also machte ich mich eines Morgens im Juli mit Rucksack, Bahnfahrkarte und einem Geldbeutel voller Euro auf den Weg und begann mein Abenteuer!

Ich nahm einen Zug von London nach Amsterdam und verbrachte ein angenehmes Wochenende, an dem ich an den Kanälen entlang radelte und köstlichen holländischen Käse probierte. Dann fuhr ich weiter nach München und erkundete den riesigen Park im Zentrum, den Englischen Garten. Als nächstes reiste ich durch die Alpen nach Lyon und dann weiter an die Westküste Frankreichs. Die Reise dauerte mehrere Tage, aber die Landschaft war so spektakulär, dass es mir nichts ausmachte. Nachdem ich in Bordeaux einen Stopp eingelegt hatte, um den berühmten Wein zu genießen, überquerte ich die Grenze nach Spanien und reiste an der Nordküste entlang, um pintxos in San Sebastián zu probieren und die Kathedrale in Santiago de Compostela zu besuchen. Mit der Straßenbahn erkundete ich die reizvolle Altstadt von Lissabon, besuchte das Prado-Museum in Madrid und lernte die außergewöhnliche Architektur von Gaudí in Barcelona kennen. Von dort kehrte ich nach Frankreich zurück und verbrachte einige Tage in den eleganten Badeorten an der Côte d'Azur.

Als ich nach Italien fuhr und in Genua ankam, wusste ich, dass meine tolle Reise fast vorbei war. Aber einen Ort musste ich noch besuchen: die historische und romantische Stadt Verona. Die Hochzeit war unglaublich schön und ich genoss eine der besten Mahlzeiten meines Lebens. Es war der perfekte Abschluss einer unvergesslichen Reise.

VOCABULARY

Die Hochzeit	wedding	**köstlich**	delicious
auf den		**erkundete**	explored
Weg machen	set off	**riesig**	huge
Der Rucksack	backpack	**Die Landschaft**	scenery
Die		**spektakulär**	spectacular
Bahnfahrkarte	rail pass	**nichts**	
angenehm	enjoyable	** ausmachen**	didn't mind
Die Kanäle	canals	**reizvolle**	charming

A tour of Europe

When I received an invitation to a wedding in Verona, Italy, I was really excited. I could take the train and go on a tour of Europe! So, one morning in July, I set off with a backpack, a rail pass, and a wallet full of euros, and began my adventure!

I took a train from London to Amsterdam and spent an enjoyable weekend cycling along the canals and trying delicious Dutch cheeses. Then I went to Munich and explored its huge central park, the Englischer Garten. Next, I traveled through the Alps to Lyon and then to the west coast of France. It took several days, but the scenery was so spectacular that I didn't mind. After stopping in Bordeaux to enjoy its famous wine, I crossed the border into Spain and traveled along the north coast, stopping to try pinxos in San Sebastián and visit the cathedral in Santiago de Compostela. I explored Lisbon's charming old town by streetcar, visited the Prado museum in Madrid, and discovered the extraordinary architecture of Gaudí in Barcelona. From there, I returned to France and spent a few days in the stylish seaside resorts of the Côte d'Azur.

When I crossed the Italian border and arrived in Genoa, I knew my amazing tour was almost over. But I had one place left to visit: the historic and romantic city of Verona. The wedding was incredible and I had one of the best meals of my life. It was the perfect end to an unforgettable trip.

VOCABULARY

kennenlernen	discovered
außergewöhnlich	extraordinary
Die Architektur	architecture
elegant	stylish
Die Badeorte	seaside resorts
unglaublich	incredible
unvergesslich	unforgettable

Answer key

Week 3

Exercise 1: 1 Der Vater liebt die Wirtin. 2 Es ist harmlos!
3 Er kauft die Zeitung. 4 Sie macht die Betten. 5 Die Tochter
holt das Auto. 6 Sie ruft die Katze und den Hund. 7 Die
Katze und der Hund kommen. 8 Die Wirtin bringt Wasser.
9 Vater, Wirtin, Tochter, Hund und Katze trinken das Wasser.

Week 4

Exercise 1: 1 Sie kaufen ein Haus und bauen Wohnungen.
2 Eine Wohnung hat keine Küche. 3 Das ist ein Problem
und sie bauen eine Küche. 4 Eine Wohnung hat kein
Wasser. 5 Das ist auch ein Problem, aber der Vater installiert
ein Wassersystem. 6 Eine Wohnung hat keinen Strom.
7 Das ist kein Problem. Der Sohn ist Elektriker. 8 Eine
Wohnung hat eine Küche, Wasser, Strom und (einige)
Schränke, aber keine Fenster. 9 Das ist kein Problem, es ist
eine Katastrophe.

Exercise 2: 2 Zwei Brote kosten €5 (fünf Euro).
3 Zwei Würste kosten €3 (drei Euro). 4 Zwei Uhren kosten
€170,00 (hundertsiebzig Euro). 5 Zwei Zeitungen kosten
€3,50 (drei Euro fünfzig). 6 Zwei Betten kosten €688
(sechshundertachtundachtzig Euro). 7 Zwei Schränke kosten
€1 010 ((ein)tausendzehn Euro). 8 Zwei Messer kosten
€7,20 (sieben Euro zwanzig). 9 Zwei Rosen kosten €4,30
(vier Euro dreißig). 10 Zwei Autos kosten €36 000,00
(sechsunddreißigtausend Euro).

Exercise 3: Ich bringe meinem Vater ein Buch. Ich gebe es
ihm im Flur. Ich schenke meinem Bruder einen Hund und
wünsche ihm einen guten Tag.

Week 5

Exercise 1: 1 Was 2 Wann 3 Wen 4 Wo 5 Wer 6 Wie
7 Warum

Exercise 2:

Verkäufer	Bitte schön …?
Fremde	Guten Tag. Haben Sie einen Führer?
Verkäufer	Was für einen Führer?
Fremde	Einen Stadtführer.
Verkäufer	Ich weiß es nicht. Fragen Sie bitte den Chef.
Fremde	Guten Tag. Ich suche einen Stadtführer. Haben Sie so etwas?
Chef	Ja sicher. Die Stadtführer sind drüben. Gucken Sie dort …
Fremde	Es ist verrückt. Ich finde Stadtführer von Frankfurt, Gießen, Marburg und Kassel, aber ich finde keinen Stadtführer von Bunsenheim.
Chef	Natürlich nicht. Warum brauchen wir Stadtführer von Bunsenheim? Wir wohnen hier und kennen die Stadt!

Exercise 3: 2 größer 3 jünger 4 klüger 5 wärmer
6 länger 7 netter

Week 6

Exercise 1: Der Verbrecher steht mit einem Pinsel und einer Palette in der Hand vor einem Bild. Auf dem Bild sind mehrere Sachen. Auf einer Tischdecke liegt ein Brot, neben dem Brot ist ein Glas und hinter dem Brot ist eine Flasche mit einem Korken. Auf der Flasche ist ein Etikett. Was ist aber für den Verbrecher am wichtigsten? Die Feile in dem/im Brot natürlich!

Exercise 2: Der Einbrecher geht bis an die Haustür. Er klopft an die Tür. Niemand kommt zur Tür. Er geht um das Haus und guckt durch die Fenster. Er findet ein Auto ohne Nummernschild zwischen dem Haus und der Garage.

Er geht zurück an die Haustür. Er steckt eine Feile zwischen die Tür und den Rahmen. Er öffnet die Tür mit der Feile und geht in den Flur. Ihm gegenüber auf der Treppe sitzt ein Skelett mit einer Axt in der Hand!

Exercise 3:

Hotelgast	Was gibt es im Fernsehen heute Abend?
Kellner	Ich weiß es nicht.
Hotelgast	Gucken Sie bitte in die Fernsehzeitung.
Kellner	Es gibt keine Fernsehzeitung diese Woche.
Hotelgast	Gibt es eine Tageszeitung?
Kellner	Ja, hier ist eine Tageszeitung … aber sie ist leider von gestern.

Week 7

Exercise 1: 2 Nein, sie ist mit ihrer Schwester bei Müllers eingeladen. 3 Nein, der Vater kommt ohne unser Geschenk für die Mutter. 4 Nein, ich esse den Kuchen mit einer Tasse Kaffee. 5 Nein, er geht mit seinem Stadtführer durch Frankfurt. 6 Nein, ich mache das Abendbrot ohne meine Tochter. 7 Nein, sie geht ohne ihren Bruder zur Tante. 8 Nein, wir kaufen die Wurst ohne eine Cola.

Exercise 2: 1 Keiner, (Jeder) 2 Welche 3 Keinen, Diesen 4 Keinen, Diesen 5 (Jeder), Dieser 6 Solches, Welches 7 Welches 8 Jeder, Dieser 9 Welche, Jede

Translation of conversation:

Her	Could you go and do the shopping now?
Him	Certainly! Do you have a shopping list for me?
Her	No, I'll tell you everything … First please pick up a small white loaf and ten fresh rolls from the baker's.
Him	They're cheaper at the supermarket, and we're going there this afternoon.
Her	All right. Then buy half a pound of ground meat and 350 grams of boiled ham at the butcher's.

Him   They always serve me badly at the butcher's.
I would rather buy meat in the old town, and we also have to go there this afternoon.
Her   Okay. Then from the produce stand I need lettuce, one and a half pounds of small, firm tomatoes, a nice cucumber, ten pounds of potatoes, and a pound of French beans.
Him   The things for the salad and the other vegetables aren't urgent, and after all there's (a) market tomorrow.
Her   Fine, but I definitely need eggs.
Him   No, you don't need (them). We still have a lot.
We'll get eggs from the market too.
Her   All right, then you don't need to go shopping.

Exercise 4: 2 Hol bitte ein kleines Weißbrot vom Bäcker. Das Weißbrot kaufe ich lieber im Supermarkt. 3 Hol bitte 250 Gramm gekochten Schinken vom Metzger. Den gekochten Schinken kaufe ich lieber in der Altstadt. 4 Hol bitte einen Kopfsalat vom Gemüsegeschäft. Den Kopfsalat kaufe ich lieber auf dem Markt. 5 Hol bitte zwanzig Eier. Die Eier kaufe ich lieber auf dem Markt. 6 Hol bitte eine schöne Gurke vom Gemüsegeschäft. Die Gurke kaufe ich lieber auf dem Markt. 7 Hol bitte zehn frische Brötchen vom Bäcker. Die Brötchen kaufe ich lieber im Supermarkt. 8 Hol bitte ein halbes Pfund Hackfleisch vom Metzger. Das Hackfleisch kaufe ich lieber in der Altstadt. 9 Hol bitte zehn Pfund Kartoffeln vom Gemüsegeschäft. Die Kartoffeln kaufe ich lieber auf dem Markt. 10 Hol bitte ein Pfund grüne Bohnen vom Gemüsegeschäft. Die grünen Bohnen kaufe ich lieber auf dem Markt.

Week 8

Exercise 1: 1 kann 2 müssen 3 darf 4 muss 5 darf 6 darf
7 kann

Exercise 2: 1 damit 2 darauf 3 danach 4 dazu 5 dafür
6 daneben 7 dagegen 8 dazwischen 9 dahinter 10 davor

Exercise 3: 1 tue/stelle 2 sind/liegen 3 tue/lege 4 tun/
stellen 5 tue/stelle 6 sind/stehen 7 tue/lege 8 tue/stecke
9 tue/lege 10 ist/liegt 11 sind/liegen 12 tue/lege 13 tue/stelle

Exercise 4: Now look! I'll clear out the fridge as much as possible. Then you'll be able to find everything quite easily. I'm putting the chicken for Sunday, the frozen raspberry flan, and the two oven-ready meals into the freezer. You can eat the oven-ready meals tomorrow and the day after. The plum tart and the dish with cream are at the top. I'm also putting the two bottles of wine there … Oh, there's just a little space there still, I can put the carton of yogurt in between. I'm putting the four bottles of beer in the bottom of the door, and two cartons of milk are next to them. I'm putting the packet of boiled ham, the salami, and the liver sausage in the middle. They're for evenings, obviously … Eggs? … I'm putting the eggs singly in the top of the door, of course, twelve of them. I'm putting two sticks of butter in the top compartment in the door. I'll leave the third one out to get soft. The flat container with three sorts of cheese is in the middle, and a container of mayonnaise and the sliced cheese are behind it. The cucumber, lettuce, grapes, and tomatoes are at the bottom, and I'm putting the bag of oranges, one cauliflower, and the sprouts in the vegetable drawer right at the bottom. I'll put a little jar of honey and a jar of strawberry jam a little higher in the door … My goodness, how full the fridge is again!

Week 9

Exercise 1: 1 denen 2 der 3 dem 4 das 5 der 6 das 7 den 8 die 9 denen 10 dem

Exercise 2: 1 hat/gebracht 2 ist/geflogen 3 sind/gestorben 4 hat/gestellt 5 ist/gesprungen 6 bin/geblieben 7 ist/gestiegen 8 habe/geschickt 9 haben/bekommen 10 bist/geworden

Exercise 3: 1 (b) 2 (c) 3 (a) 4 (b) 5 (a) 6 (c)

Week 10

Exercise 1: Ich habe vor, eine Party zu geben. Wir sind so viele, also richte ich meine Wohnung anders ein. Ich lade nur meine besten Freunde ein, aber wir sind fünfzig. Diesmal helfen meine Freunde mal nicht mit. Ich will alles alleine machen. Um 8 Uhr rufe ich sie an. Dann können sie kommen. Aber was sagen meine Freunde, sie schlagen stattdessen vor, gar nicht zu essen, sondern den ganzen Abend lang zu tanzen.

Exercise 2: 2 Anja steht früh auf, um mit ihrem Hund spazieren zu gehen. 3 Mittags kommt sie nach Hause und arbeitet im Garten, statt zu essen. 4 Am Nachmittag geht sie ins Kino, ohne jemanden zu fragen. 5 Sie sieht gerne Filme, um auf andere Gedanken zu kommen. 6 Am Abend kommt ihr Freund, um sie ins Restaurant einzuladen. 7 Sie verlässt das Restaurant während des Essens, ohne zu bezahlen. 8 Er bleibt im Restaurant sitzen und isst beide Portionen, statt seiner Freundin zu folgen.

Week 11

Exercise 1: 2 …, dass Martin solche Vorschläge nicht machen soll. 3 …, dass Paul endlich mal etwas tun soll. 4 …, dass er sein Handgelenk plötzlich verletzt. 5 …, dass er Paul zum Arzt schickt. 6 …, dass Paul einfach faul ist!

Exercise 2: 2 Nachdem man gegessen hat, soll man eigentlich nicht schlafen. 3 Während man isst, darf man nicht zu viel reden. 4 Obwohl er viel geredet hat, hat er eigentlich nicht viel gesagt. 5 Weil das Wetter schön ist, müssen wir endlich im Garten arbeiten. 6 Bis das Programm anfängt, kannst du noch schön in der Küche helfen! 7 Weil du hohen Blutdruck hast, musst du weniger arbeiten. 8 Obwohl er starke Schmerzen hat, läuft er jeden Tag.

Week 12

Exercise 1: 2 Während Alex im Garten arbeitete, hat sich sein Bruder Musik angehört. 3 Während Hanna einen Brief schrieb, ist ihre Freundin schwimmen gegangen. 4 Während Markus Milch trank, hat sein Bruder Anton Wasser getrunken. 5 Während Frau Krause mit ihrem Nachbarn sprach, hat ein Einbrecher ihr Geld vom Küchentisch gestohlen. 6 Während sich die Eltern oben im Haus stritten, haben die Kinder unten im Haus eine Party gehalten. 7 Während Emil mit den Eltern sprach, hat Lea den Hund eingefangen.

Exercise 2: 2 (a) Wenn du die Fahrkarte besorgen würdest, dann hätten wir die Möglichkeit, am Wochenende in die Berge zu fahren. (b) Würdest du die Fahrkarte besorgen, dann hätten wir die Möglichkeit, am Wochenende in die Berge zu fahren. 3 (a) Wenn Peter nicht das Fenster schließt, dann wird es zu kalt für uns alle. (b) Schließt Peter nicht das Fenster, dann wird es zu kalt für uns alle. 4 (a) Wenn dieser Mann nicht den Club verlässt, dann wird es Krach geben. (b) Verlässt dieser Mann nicht den Club, dann wird es Krach geben. 5 (a) Wenn die kleine Tochter nicht fernsehen dürfte, dann wäre sie schwierig. (b) Dürfte die kleine Tochter nicht fernsehen, dann wäre sie schwierig. 6 (a) Wenn der Vater in die Kneipe geht, dann sitzt er immer draußen. (b) Geht der Vater in die Kneipe, dann sitzt er immer draußen. 7 (a) Wenn du jetzt das Essen für Sonntag kochst, dann wirst du am Sonntagmorgen schlafen können. (b) Kochst du jetzt das Essen für Sonntag, dann wirst du am Sonntagmorgen schlafen können.

Week 13

Exercise 1: 2 Jedoch bucht Emil eine Fahrt nach Berlin. Emil bucht jedoch eine Fahrt nach Berlin. (trotzdem, allerdings) 3 Allerdings gibt es sehr viele Touristen. Es gibt allerdings sehr viele Touristen. (deshalb, jedoch, außerdem) 4 Andererseits gibt es in Berlin viel zu sehen. In Berlin gibt es andererseits viel zu sehen. (jedoch) 5 Außerdem ist es historisch und politisch wichtig. Es ist außerdem historisch und politisch wichtig. (andererseits) 6 Immerhin war es vor einiger Zeit das Tor zwischen Westen und Osten. Es war immerhin vor einiger Zeit das Tor zwischen Westen und Osten. 7 Trotzdem hat er Berlin sehr interessant gefunden. Er hat trotzdem Berlin sehr interessant gefunden. (jedoch, allerdings, andererseits)

Exercise 2: 1 (a) 2 (c) 3 (b) 4 (b) 5 (b) 6 (c) 7 (c)

Mini-dictionary

In this mini-dictionary, the plural form of a noun is given in brackets. After a verb, (I) indicates TYPE I (inseparable prefix) verbs; (II) indicates TYPE II (separable prefix) verbs. For the numbers in German, see sections 4.2 and 7.4.

GERMAN–ENGLISH

ab und zu occasionally
der **Abend (-e)** evening
das **Abendbrot (-e)** dinner
abends in the evenings
die **Abendveranstaltung (-en)** evening entertainment/event
aber but
der **Abfall (-̈e)** rubbish, waste
abgesehen (davon) apart (from that)
abhängen (II) (von) to depend (on)
abholen (II) to collect, pick up
abhören (II) to listen to, check (e.g. heart)
abnehmen (II) to lose weight
der **Abzug (-̈e)** print, copy
Ach! Oh!
achten (auf) to pay attention (to), keep an eye (on)
die **Ahnung (-en)** idea, clue, notion
all all
alle zwei Tage every other day
allein(e) alone
allerdings admittedly, mind you, ... though
alles everything
das **Allgäu** (mountainous area in Southern Bavaria)
allgemein general, in general
als than, as, when
also so, therefore, well
alt old
das **Alter (-)** age
die **Altstadt** old (part of) town
am = an dem

an at, on, to, by, on to, up to
anbieten (II) to offer
anderer, etc. other, different
andererseits on the other hand
ändern to change, alter
anderthalb one and a half
der **Anfang (-̈e)** beginning, start
anfangen (II) to begin, start
der **Anfänger (-) / die Anfängerin (-nen)** beginner
die **Angelegenheit (-en)** matter, affair, business
angenehm pleasant
die **Angst (-̈e)** fear, anxiety, worry
anhalten (II) to stop, pull up
anhören (II) sich to listen to, sound
ankommen (II) to arrive
anrufen (II) to call, telephone
anschaffen (II) to get, acquire, obtain, buy
die **Ansicht (-en)** view, opinion
ansonsten otherwise, apart from that
anstatt instead (of)
anstrengend strenuous, energetic, exhausting
antworten to answer
anziehen (II) to put on (clothes)
anziehen (II) sich to get dressed
die **Apfelsine (-n)** orange
der **April** April
arabisch Arabic

arbeitslos unemployed
ärgern sich to get annoyed
arm poor
der **Arzt** (¨e) / die **Ärztin** (-nen) doctor
auch also, too, even
auf on, on top of, on to
der **Aufkleber** (-) sticker
aufkommen (II) to (be liable to) pay
aufmachen (II) to open
die **Aufnahme** (-n) exposure, photo, shot
aufnehmen (II) to accept, admit
aufpassen (II) to pay attention, take note, watch
aufregen (II) sich to get excited/worked up
der **Aufschnitt** sliced (cold) meat
aufstehen (II) to get up
auftauchen (II) to turn up, appear
der **Augenblick** (-e) moment
im Augenblick/ augenblicklich at the moment
der **August** August
aus out of, from
der **Ausflug** (¨e) excursion, outing
ausgeben (II) to spend
ausgehen (II) to go out
aushängen (II) to post, put up, display
der **Ausländer** (-) / die **Ausländerin** (-nen) foreigner
der **Auslöser** (-) shutter release
ausmachen (II) to put out, switch off
aussehen (II) to look, appear
außerdem besides, moreover, furthermore
außerhalb outside (of)
äußerst extremely
die **Aussicht** (-en) view, prospect

aussuchen (II) to choose, select
austauschen (II) to exchange
auswechseln (II) to replace
ausziehen (II) sich to get undressed
das **Auto** (-s) car
der **Automat** (-en noun) vending machine
die **Axt** (¨e) ax

der **Bäcker** (-) / die **Bäckerin** (-nen) baker
baden to bathe, swim
der **Bahnhof** (¨e) station
bald soon
die **Banane** (-n) banana
die **Bar** (-s) bar
bauen to build
der **Bauer** (-n noun) / die **Bäuerin** (-nen) farmer
der **Baum** (¨e) tree
der **Becher** (-) cup, mug, carton
bedanken (I) sich to say thank you, express thanks
bedeuten (I) to mean
bedienen (I) to serve
bedrohen (I) to threaten
beeilen (I) sich to hurry (up)
befinden (I) sich to be situated
begegnen (I) to meet
behalten (I) to keep
der **Behälter** (-) container
behandeln (I) to treat
bei with, at, in
beide, etc. both, two
das **Beisammensein** being with people, get-together
beitreten (II) to join
bekannt known, well-known, acquainted
der/die **Bekannte** (adj.) acquaintance
beklagen (I) sich to complain
bekommen (I) to get, obtain
bemerken (I) to notice

benutzen (I) to use
der Berg (-e) mountain, hill
der Beruf (-e) job, trade, profession, occupation
beschränken (I) to limit, restrict
beschweren (I) **sich** to complain
der Besitzer (-) / **die Besitzerin** (-nen) proprietor, owner
besonder, etc. special
besonders especially
besorgen (I) to get, obtain
besprechen (I) to discuss, talk over
besser better
bestehen (I) (auf) to insist (on)
bestellen (I) to order
die Bestellung (-en) order
(am) besten best of all
bestimmt definite
besuchen (I) to visit, attend
betrinken (I) **sich** to get drunk
das Bett (-en) bed
der Beutel (-) bag
bevor before
bewegen (I) **sich** to move
bezahlen (I) to pay for
das Bier beer
bieten to offer
das Bild (-er) picture, photograph
billig cheap, inexpensive
der Bindfaden string
bis until, up to
(ein) bisschen a bit
bist (you) are (inf. sing.)
bitte please
Bitte schön? Can I help you?
Bitte schön! Here you are!
bitten (um) to ask (for), request
blass pale
der Bleistift (-e) pencil
blenden to dazzle
die Blume (-n) flower

das Blumengeschäft (-e) florist's
der Blumenkohl cauliflower
der Blutdruck blood pressure
bluten to bleed
die Blutprobe (-n) blood test
der Boden (÷) floor, ground
die Bohne (-n) bean
böse angry, naughty, wicked
brauchen to need
brechen to break
breit wide
brennen to burn
der Brief (-e) letter
bringen to bring, take
das Brot (-e) bread, loaf
das Brötchen (-) roll
der Bruder (÷) brother
das Buch (÷er) book
der Buchstabe (-ns noun) letter (of the alphabet)
der Bus (-se) bus
die Butter butter

der Cent (-s) cent
die Chance (-n) chance
checken to check
der Chef (-s) / **die Chefin** (-nen) boss
die CD-Hülle CD case
der Club (-s) club
der Cousin (-s) / **die Cousine** (-n) cousin

da there, then, as
das Dach (÷er) roof
dafür for it, instead
dagegen against it, on the other hand
daher from there, therefore
dahin (to) there
dahinter behind it
damals then, at that time
die Dame (-n) lady
damit with it, in order that, so that

danach after that, afterward
daneben next to it
Danke(schön)! Thank you!
dann then
darüber over it, above it,
  about it
darum about this, therefore, so
das the (neuter), that
dauern to last
davor before it
dazu to it, with it
dazwischen between them
die **Decke (-n)** ceiling
der **Defekt (-e)** fault
denken to think
denn for, as, since, then
dennoch nevertheless, yet
der/die/das, etc. the, that
deren whose, of whom
derselbe, etc. the same
deshalb therefore
dessen whose, of whom
deswegen on account of it,
  therefore
der **Deutscher / die Deutsche**
  German man/woman, people
der **Dezember** December
das **Dia (-s)** slide
dich you (inf. sing.)
der **Dienstag** Tuesday
dieser, etc. this
dir to/for you (inf. sing.)
der **Direktor (-en) / die**
  Direktorin (-nen) director
doch but, however, after all
der **Donnerstag** Thursday
das **Doppelzimmer (-)**
  double room
dort there
dorthin (to) there
die **Dose (-n)** can, jar
draußen outside
das **Drittel (-)** third
drüben over there
der **Druck (¨e)** pressure

drücken to press
du you (inf. sing.)
dumm silly, stupid
dunkel dark
durch through, by
dürfen may, to be
  allowed to/able to
die **Dusche (-n)** shower
duzen to use "du"

eben just, just now, simply
ebenfalls likewise
ebenso just as
die **Ecke (-n)** corner
egal all the same, regardless
ehemalig former
das **Ei (-er)** egg
eigen own
eigentlich really, actually
eilen to be urgent
ein, etc. a, one
einbegriffen included
einbilden (II) sich to imagine
der **Einbrecher (-) / die**
  Einbrecherin (-nen) burglar
einfach simple
eingeladen invited
einige, etc. some, a few
einkaufen (II) to do the
  shopping
die **Einkaufsliste (-n)** shopping
  list
einladen (II) to invite
einmal once
einnehmen (II) to eat, take,
  consume
einrichten (II) to furnish,
  arrange
der **Eintritt (-e)** admission
einverstanden agreed
einwandfrei perfect, flawless
einzeln separate, one by one
das **Einzelzimmer (-)** single room
das **Eisfach (¨er)** freezer
  compartment

elegant elegant

der **Elektriker (-) / die Elektrikerin (-nen)** electrician

empfehlen (I) to recommend

empfinden (I) to feel

endlich finally, at last

enthalten (I) to contain, include

die **Entscheidung (-en)** decision

entschuldigen (I) sich to apologize

Entschuldigung! Excuse me!

die **Entschuldigung (-en)** excuse, apology

entsprechen (I) to correspond

er he

(meines) Erachtens in my opinion

die **Erdbeermarmelade** strawberry jam

der **Erfolg (-e)** success

die **Erfrischung (-en)** refreshment

das **Ergebnis (-se)** result

erinnern (I) sich (an) to remember

erkälten (I) sich to catch a cold

erkältet sein to have a cold

die **Erkältung (-en)** cold

erscheinen (I) to appear

ersetzen (I) to replace

erst first, only

erwarten (I) to expect, await

erzählen (I) to tell, relate

die **Erziehung** education, upbringing

es it

essen to eat

das **Essen (-)** food, meal

das **Etikett (-en)** label

etwa approximately, perhaps

etwas something

   so etwas something/anything like that

euch you (inf. pl.)

euer your (inf. pl.)

der **Euro (-s)** euro

das **Exemplar (-e)** copy

das **Experiment (-e)** experiment

der **Export (-e)** export

extra extra, on purpose, deliberately

das **Fach (-̈er)** compartment, subject

fahren to go (by means of transportation), travel

die **Fahrkarte (-n)** ticket

das **Fahrrad (-̈er)** bicycle

die **Fahrt (-en)** journey, trip

fallen to fall

falls in case

falsch wrong

fangen to catch

die **Farbe (-n)** color, paint

der **Februar** February

der **Fehler (-)** mistake, error

feiern to celebrate

die **Feile (-n)** file

das **Fenster (-)** window

die **Ferien (pl.)** holiday(s)

das **Fernsehen / der Fernseher** television

die **Fernsehzeitung (-en)** TV magazine

fertig ready, finished

das **Fertigessen (-)** oven-ready meal

fest firm

das **Festessen (-)** banquet

das **Feuer (-)** fire

das **Feuerwerk** fireworks

fies nasty

die **Figur (-en)** figure

der **Film (-e)** film

finanzieren to finance

finden to find

der **Fisch (-e)** fish

flach flat, shallow

die **Flasche (-n)** bottle

das **Fleisch** meat
fliegen to fly
fliehen to flee
der **Fliesenleger (-)** / **die**
Fliesenlegerin (-nen) tiler
flirten to flirt
der **Flur (-e)** hall
die **Folge (-n)** consequence
folgen to follow
der **Fotoapparat (-e)** camera
die **Frage (-n)** question
in Frage kommen
to be possible
nicht in Frage kommen
to be out of the question
fragen to ask
der **Franzose (-n noun)** /
die Französin (-nen)
French man/woman
französisch French
die **Frau (-en)** woman, wife, Mrs.
frech insolent, bold
frei free, vacant
freihalten (II) to keep clear
freilich admittedly, to be sure
der **Freitag** Friday
freuen sich auf to look
forward to
freuen sich (über) to be
pleased/glad (about)
der **Freund (-e)** / **die Freundin**
(-nen) friend, boy/girlfriend
freundlich kind, friendly
frisch fresh
froh glad
die **Frucht (-̈e)** fruit
früh early
früher earlier, former(ly)
der **Frühling** spring
das **Frühstück** breakfast
fühlen sich to feel
der **Führer (-)** / **die Führerin**
(-nen) guide, leader
der **Führerschein (-e)** driver's
license

der **Fünfzigeuroschein (-e)** fifty
euro note
funktionieren to work,
function
für for
furchtbar terrible, frightful,
fearful
fürchten sich (vor) to be
afraid (of)

ganz all, whole
gar nicht not at all
gar nichts nothing at all
die **Garage (-n)** garage
der **Garten (-̈)** garden
der **Gast (-̈e)** / **die Gästin (-nen)**
guest, visitor
(fem. form is rare)
das **Gasthaus (-̈er)** inn, hotel
die **Gaststube (-n)** lounge
(of inn/hotel)
geben to give
es gibt there is/are
der **Geburtstag (-e)** birthday
der **Gedanke (-ns noun)** thought
geduldig patient
geeignet suitable, suited
gefährlich dangerous
gefallen (I) to please
der/die **Gefangene (adj.)** prisoner
gefroren frozen
gegen against, toward
die **Gegend (-en)** area, region,
neighborhood
das **Gegenteil** opposite
gegenüber opposite
gegenzeichnen (II) to
countersign
gehen to go, walk
es geht um it's about
Wie geht's? How's it going?
gehören (I) to belong
gekocht boiled, cooked
gelb yellow
das **Geld** money

die **Gelegenheit (-en)** opportunity

das **Gelenk (-e)** joint

gelingen (I) to succeed

das **Gemüse** vegetables

das **Gemüsefach (¨er)** vegetable compartment

das **Gemüsegeschäft (-e)** greengrocer's

genau exact, precise

genieren sich to be embarrassed

genießen (I) to enjoy

genug enough

genügend enough, sufficient

das **Gepäck** luggage

gerade just, just now

gerade erst only just

geradeaus straight ahead

  immer geradeaus (gehen) to keep (going) straight ahead

das **Gerät (-e)** machine, (piece of) equipment

gern gladly

das **Geschäft (-e)** business, shop

geschehen (I) to happen

geschlossen closed

der **Geschmack (¨e or ¨er)** taste

die **Geschwister (pl.)** brother(s) and/or sister(s)

gesellig sociable

der **Gesellschaftsraum (¨e)** lounge

gestern yesterday

gesund healthy

das **Getränk (-e)** drink

gewachsen sein to be able to cope with

gewiss certainly

das **Gewitter (-)** thunderstorm

gewöhnen (I) sich (an) to get used/accustomed (to)

das **Glas (¨er)** glass, jar

der **Glaube (-ns noun)** belief

glauben to believe, think

gleich straight away, immediately, at once, same, similar

das **Glück** luck, happiness

golden gold, golden

das **Gramm (-e)** gram

gratulieren to congratulate

(es) graut mir (vor) I have a horror (of)

die **Grenze (-n)** frontier, border

grillen to grill

groß big, large, tall

die **Größe (-n)** size

der **Großvater (¨)** / die **Großmutter (¨)** grandfather / grandmother

der **Grundpreis (-e)** basic price

die **Gruppe (-n)** group

grüßen to greet, wave

  Grüß Gott! Hello!

gucken to look, peep

gut good, well

  Guten Abend/Morgen/Tag! Good evening/morning/day!

  Meine Güte! My goodness!

  Na gut. All right then.

haben to have

das **Hackfleisch** minced meat

das **Hähnchen (-)** chicken

halb half

die **Hälfte (-n)** half

Hallo! Hello!

halt just, simply

halten to hold

halten (von) to think (of/about)

die **Hand (¨e)** hand

der **Handball** handball

handeln sich um to be about

das **Handgelenk (-e)** wrist

harmlos harmless, innocuous

hart hard

hast (you) have (inf. sing.)

der **Haufen (-)** heap, pile

das Haus (¨er) house
   nach Hause (to) home
   zu Hause at home
der Hausbesitzer (-) / die
   Hausbesitzerin (-nen)
   house owner
der Hausschlüssel (-) house key,
   front door key
die Haustür (-en) front door
   heiraten to marry
   heiß hot
   heißen to be called
    das heißt that is (to say)
der Held (-en noun) /
   die Heldin (-nen) hero
   helfen to help
der Helfer (-) / die Helferin
   (-nen) assistant
   hell light, bright
   herausnehmen (II) to take out
der Herbst autumn
der Herr (-n noun, pl. -en)
   gentleman, Mr.
   herrlich splendid, glorious
das Herz (-ens noun, pl. -en)
   heart
   heute today
    heute Abend this evening
   heutzutage nowadays, now
   hier here
die Himbeertorte (-n) raspberry
   tart/flan
   hin und her backward and
   forward, to and fro
   hin und zurück there and
   back, return
   hingegen on the other hand
   hinlegen (II) sich to lie down
   hinten at the back, behind
   hinter behind
   hinterher afterward, later
der Hinweg (-e) outward journey
   historisch historic, historical
   hoch high
    am höchsten highest

die Hochzeit (-en) wedding
   hoffen to hope
   hoffentlich hopefully
   höflich polite
   holen to fetch, bring
der Honig honey
   hören to hear
das Hotel (-s) hotel
die Hülle case
der Hund (-e) dog
der Hunger hunger

   ich I
   ihm to/for him/it
   ihn him
   ihnen to/for them
   Ihnen to/for you (formal)
   ihr her, their, to/for her
   Ihr your (formal)
   immer always
    immer wieder again and
    again, repeatedly
   immerhin after all
   in in, into
   indem by
die Inflation inflation
   infolgedessen consequently
   informieren to inform
   inklusive inclusive
   innerhalb inside of
   installieren to install
das Instrument (-e) instrument
   interessant interesting
   interessieren to interest
   interessieren sich (für) to be
   interested (in)
   interessiert (an) interested (in)
   irgendein some or other, any
   irgendwo somewhere,
   anywhere
   ist is

   ja yes, of course
das Jahr (-e) year
   jahrelang for years

der **Januar** January
Jawohl! Certainly!
je each, ever
jedenfalls at any rate
jeder, etc. every, each, any
jedoch however
jemals ever
jemand, etc. someone
jener, etc. that
jenseits on the far side (of), beyond
jetzt now
jeweils each time
das **Joghurt (-s)** yogurt
der **Juli** July
jung young
der **Junge (-n noun, pl. -n)** boy
der **Juni** June

der **Kaffee** coffee
die **Kalorie (-n)** calorie
kalt cold
kaputt broken (down), exhausted
die **Karotte (-n)** carrot
die **Kartoffel (-n)** potato
der **Käse** cheese
der **Kassenbon (-s)** sales receipt
die **Katastrophe (-n)** catastrophe
die **Katze (-n)** cat
der **Kauf (¨-e)** purchase
kaufen to buy
kaum scarcely, hardly
kein not a, no, not any
der **Kellner (-) / die Kellnerin (-nen)** waiter / waitress
kennen to know (someone, a place, object, etc.)
das **Kind (-er)** child
der **Kinderarzt (¨-e) / die Kinderärztin (-nen)** pediatrician
das **Kino (-s)** movie theater
die **Kirche (-n)** church
klagen to complain

die **Klarinette (-n)** clarinet
der/die **Klassenbeste (adj.)** best in the class
der **Klassenkamerad (-en noun) / die Klassenkameradin (-nen)** classmate
das **Klavier (-e)** piano
der **Klavierlehrer (-) / die Klavierlehrerin (-nen)** piano teacher
das **Kleid (-er)** dress
klein small, little
klingen to sound
klopfen to knock
klug clever
die **Kneipe (-n)** bar
der **Koffer (-)** suitcase
der **Kohl** cabbage
der **Komfort** comfort
kommen to come
kommen zu to happen
die **Konferenz (-en)** conference
können can, to be able to
kontrollieren to check
das **Konzert (-e)** concert
der **Kopf (¨-e)** head
der **Kopfsalat** lettuce
der **Korken (-)** cork
kosten to cost
der **Krach** noise, racket, quarrel
krank ill, sick
die **Krankheit (-en)** illness, disease
die **Kreuzung (-en)** crossroads, junction, intersection
kriechen to creep, crawl
kriegen to get
die **Kritik (-en)** criticism
die **Küche (-n)** kitchen
der **Kuchen (-)** cake
der **Kühlschrank (¨-e)** fridge
der **Kunde (-n noun) / die Kundin (-nen)** customer
die **Kusine (-n)** female cousin
der **Kurs (-e)** course, exchange rate
kurz short

kurz danach shortly after
kurz davor shortly before
lachen to laugh
landen to land
lang(e) long
langsam slow
langweilig boring
lassen to let, make, leave
laufen to run, walk
laut loud, noisy
lecker tasty, delicious
leer empty
legen to put, lay (flat)
der Lehrer (-) / die Lehrerin
  (-nen) teacher
leicht easy
leiden to suffer
leider unfortunately, (to be)
  sorry (that)
leihen to lend, borrow
leisten to achieve, manage,
  accomplish
lesen to read
letztens recently, lately
die Leute (pl.) people
das Licht (-er) light
die Liebe (-n) love
lieben to love
lieber rather
das Lieblingsreiseziel (-e)
  favourite destination
liegen to lie, be (situated)
liegen lassen to leave (lying)
  about/behind
die Limonade (-n) lemonade
losfahren (II) to set out, come
  out, drive off
loslassen (II) to set off
der Löwe (-n noun) lion
lügen to lie (fib)
der Luxus luxury

machen to make, do
machen sich nichts daraus
  to not worry about it

es macht nichts it doesn't
  matter
das Mädchen (-) girl
mager lean, thin
der Mai May
mal just
das Mal (-e) time, occasion
malen to paint
man one, you, people
manche, etc. quite a few, a fair
  number of
manchmal sometimes
der Mann (¨er) man, husband
manuell manual
die Manteltasche (-n) coat pocket
der Markt (¨e) market
der Marktplatz (¨e) marketplace
der März March
die Maschine (-n) machine, plane
der Maurer (-) / die Maurerin
  (-nen) bricklayer
die Mayonnaise mayonnaise
das Mehl flour
mehr more
mehrere, etc. several
mein, etc. my
meinen to think, mean, say
meinetwegen on my account,
  as far as I'm concerned
die Meinung (-en) opinion
(am) meisten most of all
der Mensch (-en noun) person,
  human being, (pl.) people
merken to notice
messen to measure
das Messer (-) knife
der Meter (-) metre
der Metzger (-) / die Metzgerin
  (-nen) butcher
mich me, myself
die Miete (-n) rent
der Mieter (-) / die Mieterin
  (-nen) tenant
die Milch milk
die Milchkanne (-n) milk jug

der **Minister (-) / die Ministerin
(-nen)** minister
misslingen (I) to fail
mit with
mitbringen (II) to bring
(with one)
mithelfen (II) to assist, help,
cooperate
das **Mitleid** sympathy, pity
das **Mittagessen (-)** lunch
die **Mitte (-n)** middle
das **Mittelmeer** Mediterranean
mitten in the middle
die **Mitternacht (⁻e)** midnight
der **Mittwoch** Wednesday
mögen may, to like
die **Möglichkeit (-en)** possibility,
opportunity
möglichst as far as possible
der **Moment (-e)** moment
im Moment at the moment
Moment mal! Just a moment!
momentan at the moment
der **Monat (-e)** month
der **Montag** Monday
morgen tomorrow
müde tired
die **Musik** music
müssen must, to have to
die **Mutter (⁻)** mother

Na gut. All right then.
nach after, to, according to
der **Nachbar (-n noun) / die
Nachbarin (-nen)** neighbor
nachdem after
nachher afterward
nachholen (II) to catch up
der **Nachmittag (-e)** afternoon
nächst next, nearest
am nächsten nearest of all
die **Nacht (⁻e)** night
der **Nachttisch (-e)** bedside table
nahe near
nähern sich to approach

nämlich namely, in fact
nass wet
natürlich naturally, of course
neben next to, alongside
nehmen to take
nein no
die **Nelke (-n)** carnation
nett nice, kind, good
das **Netz (-e)** net
neu new
das **Neujahr** New Year
das **Neujahrsfrühstück (-e)** New
Year's (Day) breakfast
der **Neujahrstag (-e)** New Year's
Day
neulich recently
nicht not
nichts nothing
nichts los nothing happening/
doing
nichts mehr no more
nie never
niedrig low
niemand, etc. no one, nobody
noch still, yet, even, nor
die **Nordsee** North Sea
der **November** November
null nought, zero, nil
das **Nummernschild (-er)**
number plate, license plate
nun now, well (now)
nur only

ob whether
oben upstairs, at the top
ober, etc. top, upper
obwohl although
oder or
offen open
offensichtlich obvious,
evident, clear
öffnen to open
oft often
ohne without
ohnehin anyway, as it is

der **Oktober** October
das **Öl** oil
das **Orchester (-)** orchestra
die **Ordnung** order
der **Orthopäde (-n noun)** /
    die **Orthopädin (-nen)**
    orthopedics specialist
der **Osten** east
    östlich east, eastern

das **Paar (-e)** pair, couple
    ein paar a few
die **Packung (-en)** pack, packet
die **Palette (-n)** palette
das **Papier (-e)** paper
    parken to park
    passen to fit, suit
    passieren to happen
der **Patient (-en noun)** /
    die **Patientin (-nen)** patient
die **Pause (-n)** break, interval,
    pause
das **Pech** bad luck
    Pech haben to be unlucky
die **Person (-en)** person
    persönlich personal
der **Pfeffer** pepper
    pfeifen to whistle
der **Pfeifton (-̈e)** whistling sound
der **Pflaumenkuchen (-)** plum
    tart
das **Pfund (-e)** pound (500 grams)
das **Picknick (-s)** picnic
der **Pinsel (-)** brush
der **Plan (-̈e)** plan
    planen to plan
der **Platz (-̈e)** place, room, space,
    seat, square
    plötzlich sudden
der **Politiker (-)** / die **Politikerin**
    (-nen) politician
    politisch political
der **Polizist (-en noun)** /
    die **Polizistin (-nen)**
    police officer

praktisch practical, handy
der **Präsident (-en noun)** /
    die **Präsidentin (-nen)**
    president
der **Preis (-e)** price
    preiswert reasonably priced
    pro per
    probieren to try
das **Problem (-e)** problem
das **Programm (-e)** program
    prüfen to test
die **Prüfung (-en)** test,
    examination
der **Pullover (-)** pullover, sweater

das **Quintett (-e)** quintet

der **Rahmen (-)** frame
    rasen to rush
    rasieren sich to shave
    raten to advise, guess
das **Rathaus (-̈er)** town hall
    rauchen to smoke
der **Raum (-̈e)** room, space
    Recht haben to be right
    rechts to/on the right
der **Rechtsanwalt (-̈e)** / die
    Rechtsanwältin (-nen)
    lawyer
die **Rede (-n)** speech, talk
    reden to speak, talk
das **Regal (-e)** shelf
    regelmäßig regular
der **Regenschirm (-e)** umbrella
    regnen to rain
    reich rich, wealthy
    reichen to pass, hand, reach
    reichhaltig varied,
    comprehensive, extensive
der **Reifen (-)** tire
die **Reihe (-n)** row, series
    reintun (II) to put in
der **Reis** rice
der **Reiseleiter (-)** / die
    Reiseleiterin (-nen) courier

der **Reisepass** (¨-e) passport
die **Reklamation** (-en)
   complaint, refund
die **Revolution** (-en) revolution
das **Rezept** (-e) recipe,
   prescription
   richtig correct, right, proper
   riechen to smell
   röntgen to X-ray
die **Rose** (-n) rose
der **Rosenkohl** Brussels sprouts
   rostig rusty
   rot red
der **Rotwein** red wine
die **Rückfahrt** (-en) return
   journey
der **Ruf** (-e) call, reputation
   rufen to call (out)
   ruhig quiet, calm

die **Sache** (-n) thing, item
   sagen to say, tell
die **Sahnesoße** (-n) cream sauce
die **Salami** salami
der **Salat** (-e) salad
das **Salz** salt
der **Samstag** Saturday
   satt full, satisfied
   sauer sour
   schaffen to manage, do, make,
   create
   schämen sich to be ashamed
der **Scheibenkäse** sliced cheese
   scheinen to seem, shine
   schenken to give (as a present)
   schicken to send
der **Schinken** (-) ham
   schlafen to sleep
das **Schlafzimmer** (-) bedroom
   schlagen to hit, beat
die **Schlagsahne** whipped cream,
   whipping cream
   schlecht bad, poor
   schließen to shut, close
   schließlich finally, after all

das **Schloss** (¨-er) lock, palace
der **Schlüssel** (-) key
   schmecken to taste (good)
der **Schmerz** (-en) pain, ache
   schmutzig dirty, filthy
   schneiden to cut
   schnell quick, fast
   schon already, even
   schön nice, lovely, pretty,
   beautiful
   schonen to spare, save
der **Schrank** (¨-e) cupboard,
   wardrobe
   schrecklich terrible, awful
   schreiben to write
der **Schuh** (-e) shoe
der **Schulanfang** (¨-e) start of
   school
die **Schuld** (-en) fault, debt
die **Schule** (-n) school
die **Schüssel** (-n) dish
   schwach weak
der **Schwager** (¨) /
   die **Schwägerin** (-nen)
   brother-in-law/sister-in-law
   schwarz black
   schwatzen gossip, chatter
   schwer heavy, serious, difficult
die **Schwester** (-n) sister
die **Schwiegertochter** (¨)
   daughter-in-law
   schwierig difficult, awkward
die **Schwierigkeit** (-en) difficulty
   schwimmen to swim
   sehen to see
   sehnen sich (nach) to long
   (for)
   sehr very
   sein to be, his, its
   seit since, for
   seitdem since (then)
die **Seite** (-n) side, page
der **Sekretär** (-e) /
   die **Sekretärin** (-nen)
   secretary

das Sektfrühstück (-e)
champagne breakfast
die Sekunde (-n) second
selber, etc. same
selbst -self, even
selten seldom, rarely
der Semmelknödel (-) dumpling
der September September
servieren to serve
die Show (-s) show
sicher sure, certain, reliable
sie she, her, they, them
Sie you (formal)
die Silvesterfahrt (-en) New
Year('s Eve) trip
das Silvesterfestessen (-) New
Year's Eve banquet
sind we/they/you (formal) are
singen to sing
sinken to sink
sitzen to sit
das Skelett (-e) skeleton
das Skifahren skiing
die Skimöglichkeit (-en)
opportunity for skiing,
(pl.) skiing facilities
so so, like this/that
so (et)was something/
anything like that
so … wie as … as
sobald as soon
sofort immediately, straight
away
der Sohn (¨e) son
solcher, etc. such
der Soldat (-en noun) /
die Soldatin (-nen) soldier
sollen should, ought to
somit therefore, thereby
der Sommer (-) summer
sondern but
der Sonderpreis (-e) special price
der Sonnabend (-e) Saturday
die Sonne sun
sonnen sich to sunbathe

der Sonntag (-e) Sunday
sonst otherwise, at other
times, or else
die Sorge (-n) worry, concern
sorgen (für) to see (to),
take care (of)
die Sorte (-n) sort, type, kind
sowieso anyway
sparen to save
die Sparsamkeit thrift, economy
der Spaß (¨e) joke, fun
Viel Spaß! Enjoy yourself!
(zu) spät late
später later, afterward
spazieren gehen to go for
a walk
spielen to play
der Sportler (-) / die Sportlerin
(-nen) sportsperson, athlete
der Sportwagen (-) sports car
sprechen to speak, talk
springen to jump
die Stadt (¨e) town
der Stadtführer (-) /
die Stadtführerin (-nen)
town guide
stammen (von/aus) to
originate (in), come (from)
stark strong
starten to start, take off
statt instead of
stattdessen instead (of that)
das Steak (-s) steak
stecken to be (situated), put
(inside), insert
stehen to stand
stehlen to steal
steif stiff
steigen to climb
die Stelle (-n) place
stellen to put, place
(upright)
sterben to die
(im) Stich lassen to leave in
the lurch

stoppen to stop, halt
stören to disturb
stoßen to bump
der **Strand (⁻e)** beach
die **Straße (-n)** street, road
streiten to quarrel
der **Strom (⁻e)** electricity
das **Stück (-e)** piece, item
der **Student (-en noun) / die Studentin (-nen)** student
studieren to study
die **Stunde (-n)** hour
stundenlang for hours
suchen to look for
der **Supermarkt (⁻e)** supermarket

der **Tag (-e)** day
  Guten Tag! Hello!
die **Tageszeitung (-en)** daily (news)paper
  tagsüber during the daytime
die **Tante (-n)** aunt
der **Tanz (⁻e)** dance
  tanzen to dance
die **Tasche (-n)** pocket
  in die Tasche greifen to dip into one's pocket
das **Taschengeld** pocket money
die **Tasse (-n)** cup
der **Teilnehmer (-) / die Teilnehmerin (-nen)** participant
das **Telefon (-e)** telephone
  telefonieren to phone
die **Telefonnummer (-n)** telephone number
das **Tennis** tennis
der **Teppich (-e)** carpet
  teuer expensive
  Wie teuer? How much?
das **Theater (-)** theatre
der **Theaterplatz** Theater Square
die **Theke (-n)** counter
die **Tiefkühltruhe (-n)** freezer
die **Tischdecke (-n)** tablecloth

die **Tochter (⁻)** daughter
die **Toilette (-n)** toilet
die **Tomate (-n)** tomato
der **Ton (⁻e)** sound, tone
das **Tor (-e)** gate, gateway, goal
der **Tourist (-en noun) / die Touristin (-nen)** tourist
die **Touristeninformation (-en)** tourist information office
tragen to carry, wear
treffen to meet
treiben to drive
trennen to separate
die **Treppe (-n)** stairs, staircase
treten to step, kick
trinken to drink
der **Tropfen (-)** drop
trotz in spite of
trotzdem in spite of (that), nevertheless
das **T-Shirt (-s)** T-shirt
die **Tube (-n)** tube
tun to do, put
die **Tür (-en)** door

über over, across, about
überdies besides
das **Übergewicht** excess weight
überhaupt in general, at all, altogether
überlassen (I) to leave
der/die **Überlebende (adj.)** survivor
übermorgen the day after tomorrow
die **Übernachtung (-en)** overnight stay
überreden (I) to persuade
die **Überstunde (-n) (pl.)** overtime
überweisen (I) to transfer
übrigens by the way
überübermorgen the day after the day after tomorrow

die **Uhr (-en)** clock, watch, o'clock, time
um around, about, at
um ... zu in order to, so as to
umgehen (II) mit to handle, deal with
der **Umzug** move, removal
unangenehm unpleasant, embarrassing
unbedingt absolute, really, without fail
unberechtigt unjustified
und and
die **Unruhe (-n)** disturbance, noise
uns (to/for) us
unser our
unsympathisch unpleasant, uncongenial
unten downstairs, at the bottom, below
unter under, below, beneath
unterbringen (II) to accommodate
die **Unterhaltung (-en)** entertainment, conversation
die **Unterkunft (-̈e)** accommodation
unterschreiben (I) to sign
untersuchen (I) to examine
unterwegs on the way
unwichtig unimportant
der **Urin** urine
der **Urlaub (-e)** holiday(s)

die **Vase (-n)** vase
der **Vater (-̈)** father
veranstalten (I) to arrange, put on
die **Veranstaltung (-en)** entertainment event
die **Verantwortung** responsibility
der **Verbrecher (-) / die Verbrecherin (-nen)** criminal
verbringen (I) to spend (time)

die **Vereinigten Staaten (pl.)** the United States
vergessen (I) to forget
das **Verhältnis (-se)** relationship; (pl.) means, circumstances
verheiratet married
verirren (I) sich to get lost
verkaufen (I) to sell
verlassen (I) to leave
verlaufen (I) sich to get lost
verletzen (I) to injure, hurt
verletzen (I) sich to get hurt
verlieren (I) to lose
der **Verlust (-e)** loss
vernünftig sensible
verrückt insane, crazy
verschieden different
verschulden (I) sich to get into debt, go into the red
versprechen (I) to promise
verstehen (I) to understand
der **Versuch (-e)** attempt
versuchen (I) to try
vertun (I) sich to make a mistake, slip up
der/die **Verwandte (adj.)** relative
verzeihen (I) to forgive, pardon
der **Vetter (-)** male cousin
viel much, a lot
viele, etc. much, many
vielleicht perhaps
das **Viertel (-)** quarter
die **Viertelstunde (-n)** quarter of an hour
voll full
vollkommen perfect
von from, of, by
vor before, in front of, ago
vorbeischauen (II) to look in
vorbereiten (II) to prepare
die **Vorbereitung (-en)** preparation
vorbeugen (II) to avert
vorfinden (II) to find, discover
vorgestern the day before yesterday

vorhaben (II) to intend, have planned

der **Vorhang (¨-e)** curtain

vorher before (that)

vorhin a little/short time ago

vorige, etc. last, previous

vorkommen (II) to happen

vornehmen (II) to undertake

vorn at the front

vorrätig in stock, to hand

vorschießen (II) to advance (money)

der **Vorschlag (¨-e)** suggestion, proposal

vorschlagen (II) to propose

der **Vorschuss (¨-e)** advance

vorsichtig careful, cautious

vorstellen (II) to introduce

vorstellen (II) sich to imagine

wachsen to grow

der **Wagen (-)** car

die **Wahl (-en)** choice, election

wahnsinnig crazy

während in the course of, during, while

währenddessen during that

wahrscheinlich probably

der **Wald (¨-er)** wood, forest

wann(?) when(?)

warm warm, hot

warten (auf) to wait (for)

warum? why?

was(?) what(?)

was = etwas

was für (ein)? what sort of (a)?

waschen to wash

waschen sich to wash, have a wash, get washed

das **Wasser** water

das **Wassersystem (-e)** plumbing, water system

weg away, gone

der **Weg (-e)** way, path

wegen on account of, because of

weggehen (II) to go away

(dabei) wegkommen (II) (mit) to get away (with)

wegwerfen (II) to throw away

weich soft

das **Weihnachten (-)** Christmas

die **Weihnachtsferien (pl.)** Christmas holiday(s)

weil because

der **Wein (-e)** wine

die **Weintraube (-n)** grape

weiß white

weiß knows

das **Weißbrot (-e)** loaf of white bread

weiter further

weiterdrehen (II) to turn on/further

welcher, etc.**(?)(!)** which(?), what(?)(!)

der **Weltkrieg (-e)** world war

wem? (to/for) whom?

wen? who(m)?

wenig little

wenige, etc. little, few

wenigstens at least

wenn if, when, whenever

wer? who?

werden will, shall, to be going to, to become

werfen to throw

wesentlich essential, significant, substantial

wessen? whose?

der **Westen** west

das **Wetter** weather

wichtig important

widersprechen (I) to contradict

wie(?) how(?)

Wie (bitte)? Pardon?

wieder again
(Auf) Wiedersehen! Goodbye!
Wieso (denn)? How's that?
Wie viel? How much?
Wie viele? How many?
der **Wille (-ns noun)** will
der **Winter (-)** winter
der **Winterprospekt (-e)** winter brochure
winzig tiny, minute
wir we
der **Wirt (-e) / die Wirtin (-nen)** landlord/landlady
wissen to know (a fact)
witzig funny, amusing
wo(?) where(?)
die **Woche (-n)** week
das **Wochenende (-n)** weekend
wohl well, probably, no doubt
wohnen to live, reside
die **Wohnung (-en)** flat, dwelling
der **Wohnwagen (-)** caravan
das **Wohnzimmer (-)** living room, lounge
der **Wohnzimmertisch (-e)** living room table
wollen to want, intend
das **Wort ("-er or -e)** word
worüber over/about which
wundern sich to be surprised
wunderschön beautiful
der **Wunsch ("-e)** wish
wünschen to wish, desire
die **Wurst ("-e)** sausage

die **Zahl (-en)** number
zahlen to pay
zählen to count
der **Zähler (-)** counter
der **Zahnarzt ("-e) / die Zahnärztin (-nen)** dentist
der **Zehneuroschein (-e)** ten euro note

zeigen to show
die **Zeit (-en)** time
vor einiger Zeit some time ago
in letzter Zeit recently
eine Zeit lang for a time
die **Zeitung (-en)** newspaper
zerstören (I) to destroy
ziehen to pull, move
ziemlich fairly, rather, pretty
das **Zimmer (-)** room
zögern to hesitate
zu to, at, too
der **Zucker** sugar
zudem besides
zufällig by (any) chance
der **Zug ("-e)** train, draught, procession
zuhören (II) to listen
die **Zündkerze (-n)** spark plug
zunehmen (II) to put on weight
zurück back
zusammen (al)together
der **Zuschlag ("-e)** surcharge
zustehen (II) to be due
zwar to be sure, admittedly
und zwar namely
zweimal twice
der **Zwilling (-e)** twin
zwischen between
das **Zypern** Cyprus

Index

The numbers refer to sections, not pages.